Answers to Your People Problems

The Christian's Guide to Good Human Relations

by John G. Kerbs

Library of Congress Catalog Card No. 68-25949
ISBN 1-57756-021-3

PREFACE

Human relations is an important factor in the life of every Christian. Practicing the principles of Christian behavior which John Kerbs sets forth in *Your People Problems* will help every reader get along better with others.

The author's interesting style of writing and many illustrations make this book highly readable. And the fact that he appears to practice what he preaches makes the high ideals which he sets forth in the field of human relations even more meaningful and acceptable to those who know the author well.

Glance through the chapter headings, read the first chapter, "Love Everybody," and I predict you will read most of the book before you put it down. Most of the chapters are short, the message of each having been put forth in a direct captivating way with little tedious sermonizing.

As with sermons, so with books—their worth can seldom be judged by length. Though this volume be small, following its helpful counsel will almost certainly draw you closer to your Saviour and to those about you.

Robert H. Pierson.

Former President of the General Conference of Seventh-day Adventists. He was the President of the South African Division when this preface was written and where the author served when he prepared the original manuscript for this book.

ABOUT THE AUTHOR

John Kerbs was born in Shattuck, Oklahoma, and is a graduate of Lodi Academy, La Sierra University, and Andrews University. At the time of the publication of this third edition, he is the president of Union College in Lincoln, Nebraska. He spent almost fifteen years in the literature ministry of the Seventh-day Adventist Church, five of those in South Africa. He was the director of literature evangelism in the South African Union Conference of Seventh-day Adventists when he prepared the original manuscript for this book.

Since that time he has been an academy and college Bible teacher and principal of Pacific Union College Preparatory School and Loma Linda Academy, both in California. Just prior to beginning his presidency of Union College in 1991, he was the Associate Dean for Admissions at Loma Linda University School of Medicine.

His wife, Nancy, teaches English as a Second Language at Union College. Their children are Jeffry, a dentist in Escondido, California; James, an orthopedic surgeon in Lexington, Ohio; and John, who died in 1983 at age 19. He was a pilot and sophomore aeronautical engineering student at California Polytechnic State University in San Luis Obispo, California.

CONTENTS

WHY STUDY
HUMAN RELATIONS?

Many feel that a study of human relations is unnecessary for the Christian, possibly because it may smack of artificiality or the use of methods to trick people into doing the things we wish them to do. But dare we be unconcerned about unsatisfactory human relationships? Jesus sets forth love, which usually, if not always, results in good human relations, as the very test of discipleship. "By this shall all men know that ye are My disciples, if ye have love one to another."[1] Whatever your profession, no person has pure love to God unless he or she has unselfish love for fellow humans. When self is merged in Christ, love springs forth spontaneously.

NO WRONG IN BEING LIKED

Though genuine goodness does not always beget the love of your fellow human beings, it is certainly right that we do all we can, without sacrificing principle, to increase "in favor with God *and* man."[2] "Especially should those who have tasted the love of Christ develop their social powers, for in this way they may win souls to the Saviour."[3]

No, the study of human relations is not wrong, but right. Its proper consideration will lead us closer to Christ, and indeed prove to be a study of the Ten Commandments in all their breadth.

J. C. Penney, the department-store magnate, said, "From the very beginning of my business career, more than half a century ago, I found that employee-employer relations based on Christian principles are harmonious and profitable. While I do not profess to have practiced them to perfection, my experience teaches me that when both employer and employee are motivated by a desire to observe Christian principles honestly, difficulties and problems are easily solved."

If human relations has to do with the observing of Christian principles in business, how much more is this true in the work of the church! Surely it is important that we study this subject.

GETTING ALONG

Some individuals congratulate themselves that they have no trouble getting along well with people generally, but there are *certain* ones with whom they cannot associate without having a quarrel. In effect this is putting the blame on the other person rather than yourself. If *she* were different, you could get along with her. R. R. Bietz once said, "To say you can't get along with someone is a sign of self-centeredness." Most of us never have "people problems" until we are with people who are *not* making an effort to get along with us. We often leave the "getting along" to the other person, and, if things don't go well, we don't like to think the fault could be with us.

NO ISLANDS

"God has invested man with an influence that makes it impossible for him to live to himself. Individually we are connected with our fellowmen, a part of God's great whole, and we stand under mutual obligations."[4] No man is an island. We cannot, nor should we desire to, escape people in this world; so each of us must come to grips with our people problems and handle them as Christ would.

This book does not profess to be an exhaustive study of problems in human relations and the reasons for their existence. The comments, quotations, and illustrations used are intended to guide you into profitable reflections upon your own "people problems," which may fall into some of the categories suggested. May you see in the discussion of each problem a call to prayer and a fuller consecration to Him who longs to dwell within us. God can make our every contact with our fellow mortals a mutual stepping-stone to a happier life here and eternal life at last.

John Kerbs.

LOVE EVERYBODY?

Trying to go to sleep one night in an already overcrowded, smoke-filled compartment on the train, I was much annoyed when the sixth man stumbled through the door smelling strongly of liquor. I was disgusted and felt he should sleep elsewhere if he insisted on drinking. I must confess I felt like telling him so and thought of asking the conductor to remove him.

No, it's not wrong to hate the smell of liquor, but I was having difficulty remembering this liquor was not in a bottle but in a child of God, a candidate for His kingdom. Finding it hard to separate the liquor from the man, I was inclined to cast both out.

God was not long in bringing me to repentance. The night was not pleasant, but I determined to do what I could to help this man. The next day, when we were alone, we had a long talk. He wept as he told of starting to drink only seven years before, of how he had lost family and job as a result. Now he was on his way to Johannesburg to seek help at a hospital for alcoholics. A man needing help—even *seeking* help—and I would have cast him out of my presence!

To add to the needed rebuke, only days after arriving in Johannesburg I received a letter which began thus: "Dear Mr. Kerbs: Many thanks for your kindness to my son on the train." The son of a praying, worrying mother! And I, who claimed to be *seeking* the lost, was almost unready to help him whom God had brought to me!

"To bend every energy toward some apparently great work, while we neglect the needy or turn the stranger from his right, is not a service that will meet His approval."[1]

MUST I LIKE EVERYONE?

Christlike human relations must take in the whole world. Will Rogers, much-loved American humorist, said, "I never met a man I didn't like." If an actor and humorist could say this, how much more should we, who claim to represent Him who "so loved the world," be able to love everyone! This is possible. As we recognize our own imperfections—and we will more and more as we draw closer to Christ—we will not dislike others because of their faults. As we dwell upon the good in people—and there is some good in everyone (even a stopped clock tells the correct time twice each day!)—making allowances for each individual's peculiar heredity and environment, we can genuinely, from the heart, like everyone.

A Christian wife, after having spent many years with an imperfect husband—which all husbands are—declared that she loved him "for his faults." This was a bit difficult for me to understand when I heard it years ago. But is it not true that with the mind of Christ[2] whose "grace did much more abound" "where sin abounded,"[3] we can come to have much affection for the person who is most faulty? Will we not find our hearts going out in a special way toward those who are most in need of love and understanding, patience and gentleness?

A MODERN MAGDALENE

Again on the train, a young woman made herself too available to the men in my compartment. A Mary Magdelene? This she made clear. What would be my reaction? The important question in this case was not concerned with our ofttimes too narrow definition of "morality." God had a finer lesson to teach me. The question soon became clear: "Will this man, this minister, who claims to be living the life of Christ, be able to reject sin *without rejecting the sinner?*" Oh, how easy it is to confuse the two and treat both sin and sinner with similar contempt!

After she learned that I was a minister, and after I read a portion of Scripture aloud, she expressed her own belief in

God. There followed a beautiful testimony of how she at the point of death had reached up and grasped the hand of God. This "sickness" had been from a self-inflicted bullet wound, one of several attempts at suicide. Her wrists were badly scarred. She sadly related the story of her impending divorce, of four nervous breakdowns, of two lovely children whom she longed for but was not permitted to keep because of her nervous condition. Though convinced that no one in this world really cared for her, she did not question the goodness of God. She wept as I prayed, and expressed gratitude for my promise to pray for her daily.

Yes, a sinner, trying to satisfy a longing for love, but nonetheless a child of God in need of help, a baby girl who had slipped from mother's arms and gone astray.

"Many have fainted and become discouraged in the great struggle of life, whom one word of kindly cheer and courage would have strengthened to overcome. . . . Never lose an opportunity to say a word to encourage and inspire hope. We cannot tell how far-reaching may be our tender words of kindness, our Christlike efforts to lighten some burden. The erring can be restored in no other way than in the spirit of meekness, gentleness, and tender love."[4]

A REWARDING EXPERIMENT

A nurse earned the nickname "Gillette" because of her cutting words, her sharp tongue. Mr. Potter, an eighty-one-year-old patient, though a very peaceable gentleman, confessed that even he smarted a bit under her treatment.

He debated the matter silently for some time and decided that perhaps there was a kindlier facet to her nature, if only one could discover it.

So Mr. Potter set out to make the discovery. He met her with a smile the next morning and asked if he had offended her in any way. She stood rigidly by his bedside frowning deeply while he offered to apologize and make amends.

His experiment was more than successful. Even he was surprised when suddenly she flung her arms about his neck and said in broken voice, "No, my dear, you have been a perfect gentleman. I have great respect for you. I know I am crabby at times and have treated you badly, but you've never retaliated like the others!"

Mr. Potter concludes, "You can't judge the marmalade by the label on the jar," and affirms that "Gillette and old Potter lived happily ever afterward!"

In mastering the fine art of human relations, we must have no misgivings in regard to the goal of loving all people—the lovely with the unlovely, the proud with the humble, the sinner with the saint. Yes, and those of another race with those of our own. The heathen with the Christian, another's children with ours, the vile with the pure, the rich *and* poor, the ignorant *and* the educated.

"Our Redeemer thirsts for recognition." And so do all His earthly children. "He hungers for the sympathy and love of those whom He has purchased with His own blood." Is it then always pride and self-centeredness in ourselves and others that cause us to also thirst for a recognition of our true worth and to hunger for sympathy and love from our fellow pilgrims on earth?[5]

CHRIST IS THE ANSWER

To put on courtesy and sweetness when we choose to can never substitute for "putting on Christ." Christ is rather to be "put in" than "put on" like a garment. He actually dwells within, and when He does there is little need for pretense. "The impulse to help and bless others springs constantly from within."[6] "When obeying Him we shall be but carrying out our own impulses."[7] To have the right kind of relations with our fellow humans we must have the experience of the apostle Paul to which he referred when he said, "I live; yet not I, but Christ liveth in me." When we have this experience we will love everybody.

| Key | HATE THE SIN, BUT LOVE THE SINNER. |

TELL IT LIKE IT IS?

"I'm afraid you're wrong there; when people are dead they're dead. They are simply dust and don't know anything." True though these words may be, they could hardly be expected to win the friendship and confidence of one who consoles himself with the thought that his loved one is in the better world.

"Your Sunday is no better than any workday. You might just as well rest on Tuesday!" This may be truth which the meticulous Sunday keeper should know, but when it is presented in this way the response will doubtless be unfavorable.

It is not always necessary or even desirable to tell people all you know, even of that which is good, right and true. Some people seem to believe that it's safe to speak if you speak the truth. But the person who follows the example of Christ will realize that there is a time to be silent even when there burns within his heart a message from heaven.

Ponder well this helpful counsel given to medical workers. Surely it applies to all workers for God. "In your work for the patients, do not allow them to receive an impression that you are intensely anxious for them to understand and to accept our faith. It is natural that there should be an intense fervency to this end. But often a wise restraint is necessary. In some cases the words that might seem appropriate would do grave injury, and close a door that might have opened wider.

"Manifest tender love, and exercise judicious forbearance. If you see a good opportunity to make a sharp point in argument, it is better often to forbear."[1]

Have you had the temptation to "tie someone in knots" when he argues, but reveals a serious lack of knowledge? We all have, I suppose, and most of us have yielded to this temptation at some time.

I met Mr. M_____ on the train. He had problems. Tears flowed as we prayed together. The fact that he agreed to prayer and subsequently shared with me his views on religion showed that I was gaining ground. I wasn't satisfied. His views were so unscriptural that I simply had to "straighten him out." I thought I was kind in my contradiction, but suddenly he turned on me in near anger: "I don't care to discuss this further! I never discuss religion or politics."

Apologies were made and we parted on friendly terms, but to some degree my overeagerness to prove a point had closed a door which might have opened wider.

WISE RESTRAINT

"Do not on all occasions present the strongest proofs you know; for this would arouse a suspicion that you were trying merely to convert your hearer to the Seventh-day Adventist faith.

"The simple Word of God has great power to convince of the truth. Let the Word speak and do its work. Let there be wise restraint in evangelistic effort. Do not force the presentation of a testing point. *Wait till inquiries are made.* Let your example teach. Let the words and works show that you believe the words of the living Teacher. (Emphasis added)"[2]

VIRTUE OR VICE

Frankness is one of those characteristics which may be either virtue or vice. While forever "beating around the bush" may be one extreme, giving to everyone the straight truth may be the other.

"There are conscientious persons who think it their duty to talk freely upon points of faith on which there is a difference of opinion, in a manner which arouses the combativeness of those with whom they converse. One such premature, injudicious effort may close the ears of one who otherwise would have heard patiently, but who will now influence others unfavorably. Thus spring up the roots of bitterness, whereby many are defiled. Through the indiscretion of one, the ears and hearts of many may be closed to the truth."[3]

NOT WORDS, BUT DEEDS

"All you ever talk about is the Sabbath," said an interested person. A rather extravagant charge? Possibly, but some of us do forget that there are some arguments for our faith more convincing than Sabbath texts.

"In times past some in the sanitarium have felt it their duty to introduce the Sabbath question in all places. They have urged it upon the patients with earnestness and persistency. To such the angels of God would say, Not *words*, but *deeds*. The daily life tells much more than any number of words. A uniform cheerfulness, tender kindness, Christian benevolence, patience, and love will melt away prejudice, and open the heart to the reception of the truth. Few understand the power of these precious influences."[4]

It may come as a surprise to some that we are not to give people the impression that we are anxious for them to become Seventh-day Adventists—to accept our faith. Did you notice in the statements above that even the presentation of the truth—that which is holy, just and good—can "do grave injury and close a door" if such presentation is made at the wrong time?

Let us never adopt the apparent belief of some who call at our doors. They seem to think a "straight from the shoulder" presentation of the gospel to anyone, anytime, anywhere is all that is necessary to leave their hearers "without excuse." Jesus timed His words carefully, realizing that there were times when His hour had not yet come. Let us do likewise.

OBNOXIOUSLY ACCURATE

It is also unwise to be "too right" in your contacts with those near to you. Have you been embarrassed and uncomfortable when your guest incessantly interrupted and corrected minor details in his wife's stories? Have you noticed her give him an icy stare or clam up? "He'll really get it when they get home!"

I've sometimes thought. Incidentally, I've been on the "getting" end once or twice myself! Have you?

Don't be so accurate that you are obnoxious. Don't interrupt and correct someone when he says "five miles" when you know the correct distance is six miles, or when he says "twenty pounds" and you know the exact figure is eighteen. After all, a story is a story, and minor inaccuracies do not constitute a lie. I believe I recall reading that someone accused Ellen White of being a false prophet because she referred to a forty-bed hospital which in reality had only thirty-nine!

If you are branded a stickler for detail, this may be a more dubious compliment than you realize.

Resist the urge to straighten people out, if there is no real principle at stake.

| Key | *BE CAREFUL—EVEN WHEN YOU KNOW YOU ARE RIGHT.* |

DO YOU TALK TOO MUCH?

"He has a screw loose!" You have heard this expression used to describe a person who is mentally unbalanced. Someone has wisely observed: "Usually the first screw that gets loose in a person's head is the one that controls the tongue."[1]

Some men of history won fame because they didn't talk much. They said little and did much.

"George Washington was one of the silent men. He talked when it was necessary, was not hesitant when directions were to be given or advice sought, but the famed Virginian was not given to small talk, nor noted as a conversationalist.

"Lincoln had his silent hours when he appeared to be withdrawn from the social chatter about him, and was not of the mind to relate incidents of old Indiana and Illinois days.

"Calvin Coolidge had a reputation as a silent President, sparing of speech. But when he was in the mood and of a mind to talk, he did not lack for words."[2]

Some of the most successful literature evangelists I have known have been very quiet, talking little and listening much. The gift of gab is often a handicap rather than a help. As someone has said, "the dog has many friends because the wag was put in his tail instead of his tongue!"

A man who talked too much made the work of Jesus more difficult. After healing a leper, Jesus "saith unto him, See thou say nothing to any man: but go thy way, show thyself to the priest. . . . But he went out, and began to publish it much, and to blaze abroad the matter, insomuch that Jesus could no more openly enter into the city, but was without in desert places."[3]

The word "blaze" in this context means: "To make known publicly; spread the news of; proclaim." There was nothing particularly wrong with the speaker, or with what was spoken, or the deed spoken of. But there was something wrong with those who heard the words of truth; and knowing there would be a wrong reaction to even that which was true, Jesus saw that silence was more desirable than speech in this case. The work of Jesus is often hindered by our speaking even the truth at the wrong place and time. We need not "blaze abroad" all that we know and think.

NO RIGHT TO TALK

Part of a rather well known prayer goes like this: "Keep me from the fatal habit of thinking I must say something on every subject and on every occasion. Release me from the craving to straighten out everybody's affairs. Make me thoughtful but not moody, helpful but not bossy. With my vast store of wisdom, it seems a pity not to use it all, but Thou knowest, Lord, that I want a few friends at the end."

The servant of the Lord warns those of us who love to talk, "Let no one lose minutes by talking when he should be working. Let the talkative man remember that there are times when he has no right to talk. . . . Have you work to do for the Master?. . . Close your lips. Make not others idle by tempting them to listen to your talk. The time of many is lost when a man uses his tongue instead of his tools."[4]

A MOUTH THREE FEET WIDE

The power of speech is a marvelous talent. But at times more effective ways than talking can be employed to get a message across. It is said truly of a certain lady that she has a mouth three feet wide, but never talks. There is no need for that. Her full name is the "Statue of Liberty Enlightening the World." Sometimes simply listening, or being, or standing for something accomplishes that which speech could not.

Key | *DON'T TALK TOO MUCH.*

SILENCE IS GOLDEN?

The idea that silence is golden can be carried too far. How many a wife is put into virtual solitary confinement by a morose husband who believes he is just the "silent type" and wants to "avoid arguments." One of the most common complaints of unhappy wives is, "He just won't talk!" Wives too can be guilty of being silent partners.

We do not mean to suggest that these silent people never talk. They usually do say something—just enough to make things worse. A sharp retort, a mumble or grumble or growl, rather than a calm, intelligent response.

WHERE'S THE MONEY GONE?

"Where have you spent all the money this month?" says wife to husband, or husband to wife.

There is probably a very satisfactory answer to this question which an hour or two of calm accounting could discover. But what happens? A brief exchange of unkind words this month, and the next, and the next. Each party too proud (or too guilty) to agree to inquiry and investigation into the perpetual problem of money shortage.

"Why are you so late tonight?"

Your answer? A cold stare to show your contempt for the insinuation that you could have been earlier.

Why be afraid to answer easy questions calmly, however stated? If it was a traffic holdup, committee, car trouble, or helping a friend, say so.

"What have you been doing all day?" Tell him. It may seem a foolish question to you, but to answer it may preclude its being asked again.

"Another new pair of shoes!" Remind him you bought your last pair ten months ago—he may really have forgotten—

instead of responding with cold, contemptuous silence.

"Why not, Daddy?"

"Because I said so!" may seem a sufficient answer to you, but is it really wrong for a child to receive a reason for your prohibitions? There always should be a reason; why not state it?

TORTUROUS SILENCE

There are times when problems or differences can be solved or cleared up only by talking them out. To sulk and refuse to talk often makes things worse. There is nothing more torturous than to be met with stolid silence when you want to make up with someone with whom you have had a quarrel.

These silent wars are not confined to the home, but have been found on the job and in the church as well.

I once saw two men in the same office not even able to exchange friendly words while they ate their lunch. I don't know yet what it was all about, but others noticed that there always seemed to be a wordless feud going on.

I witnessed a congregation meet together at least ten times to solve a problem of internal strife. At each meeting it was evident, and even stated, that the real root of the difficulty had not been disclosed. But do you think that anyone had the courage to reveal the location of the key log in this jam? There was much talking, but there was silence on that which could have guided in bringing these meetings to a quick and successful climax. How difficult an excessive amount of silence can make things!

How many courtships could end in happy marriages, how many divorces would never take place, how many only loyal mates could be genuinely happy, how many church quarrels would be cut short, and how many workers could become "workers together" again, had people only the ability to talk things over!

Key | **DON'T BE TOO SILENT.**

YOU'RE NOT LISTENING

The Greek Stoic philosopher, Epictetus, who lived in Rome during the first century A.D., said, "Nature has given to man one tongue, but two ears, that we may hear from others twice as much as we speak." And the wise man says, "Be more ready to hear. . . Let thy words be few."[1]

Most of us are extremely poor listeners. Good listening is more than just silent endurance until the other person finishes his speech so you can explain your point of view. J. C. Penney said, "Most of us think we are pretty good listeners. I know when I started out in life, I thought I was a good listener. But the longer I live, the more I realize that listening is not something that comes naturally; it is an acquired art. For most of us, listening, whether in a social conversation or around the table at a conference, is just a pause we feel obliged to grant a speaker until we again have the chance to air our own opinions.

"This is not real listening, in any sense of the word. Listening is not a passive activity during which we let our own thoughts intrude upon what someone else is saying. To listen actively to another person requires willpower, concentration, and great mental effort. Its rewards are great, because only then do we really learn something about the person—his feelings, his ambitions, his hopes, his aspirations, what kind of person he really is, what his gripes are, what his needs are.

"You'll be surprised how much more you learn from others by listening in this way once you set your mind to it, and how much it can help you in your work."

A CHRISTIAN DUTY

Yes, you will learn much by listening, but could it also be a positive Christian duty to listen well to all the people in your life, even for their sake? "Our Saviour appreciated a quiet home and interested listeners. He longed for human tenderness, courtesy, and affection."[2]

Your wife, husband, child, student, teacher, neighbor, counselee, employee, employer, fellow worker will appreciate you as an interested listener. And don't forget, "Inasmuch as ye have done it unto one of the least of these. . . ."

I LOVE PEOPLE

A literature evangelist with whom I had never canvassed before was having difficulty making sales. He said, "I just can't understand it. I love people—I just love to talk to people."

I soon learned that loving people and loving to talk to people were two different things. The bored look on this literature evangelist's face when his prospective customers were talking, his many interruptions of their comments, and the almost incessant flow of his own "wise" words proved only his love for himself. Love for people is evidenced rather by listening than by talking.

Someone said, "It takes a child two years to learn to talk and a man fifty years to learn to keep his mouth closed." And W. J. Cory in his nineteenth-century "Heraclitus," observes, "How often you and I had tired the sun with talking and sent him down the sky!"

Roche reminds us, "The surest way to excel in conversation is to listen much." Take notice, and you will see that the people with whom you like most to be, are those who not only let you talk, but actively listen and even urge you to talk by asking you questions and in other ways show an interest in what you are saying. The one whom you judge a good conversationalist will always be the good listener.

LISTEN AND SELL

The very fact that most of us like so much to talk should in itself teach us the importance of listening. An instructor of salesmen, Charles B. Roth, says, "Listen and sell. You will find that prospects like to hear themselves talk better than they like hearing you. Build on that point. Learn how to 'listen expressively.' It's not hard. You are listening expressively when you follow what your prospect says so actively and intensely that, even though you don't utter a peep, he enjoys you as an audience. You know you are 'in' as a listener when the prospect thanks you for calling and says he enjoyed visiting with you, whereas it was he who did all the talking. . . . The human side of selling, important though it is, is made up of just such trifles."

We are all selling something—ourselves, our product, our message, our books, our program, our ideas. This requires talking—and much listening.

Key | **LISTEN WELL.**

THOUGHTLESS WORDS

"If thou hast thought evil, lay thine hand upon thy mouth."[1] This text reminds us that there are no really thoughtless words. The spoken word is always preceded by a thought, either good or evil. So possibly the advice, "Think before you speak," should rather be, "Think *twice* before you speak." In fact, we may have to rethink and pray over things three or four or ten times before we can speak good words in some cases. What a different world this would be if we all possessed enough character to lay the hand upon the mouth until evil thoughts are replaced by good thoughts! "A fool uttereth all his mind: but a wise man keepeth it in till afterwards."[2]

PERFECT SPEECH OUR GOAL

We may think "Be careful little lips what you say" is for primary children, and "Let the words of my mouth . . . be acceptable in Thy sight, O Lord"[3] is for juniors. But in reality, this song and prayer , oft repeated by children, could hardly be more comprehensive and necessary for even the most mature Christian. For did not the apostle James say, "If any man offend not in word, the same is a perfect man, and able also to bridle the whole body"?[4] How important then that we be satisfied with nothing less than completely unoffensive speech.

A NEAR TRAGEDY

"What! my car not ready yet? I only wanted it greased. You said it would be ready by eleven, and it's one o'clock! I'm late already. Why didn't you tell me you couldn't do it? I'd have taken it elsewhere!"

These were my first thoughts as I saw my car just on the rack three hours after I left it at the garage. My second thoughts, however, told me, "What good will it do to censure? It's bad to be late, but why be late and also speak in an un-Christlike way? Be a gentleman."

So I kindly asked the young man under the car to hurry and went into the office to pay for the job. The one who would have received my less-than-kind words, had I acted upon my first thoughts, surprised me by asking, "Are you connected with_____ High School?"

"Well, er, no, not directly, but the church I belong to operates it."

"Do you know anything about _____ Elementary School?" she continued.

"Not too much, but it's also our school."

"Are you going to send your children there?" she questioned further.

"Why, yes, my eldest son will be there next year. Are you interested in these schools?" I queried.

I learned her eldest son had begun attending our boarding academy but was rather unhappy and wanted to come home. From our conversation it was obvious she was in the balance—should she bring him home or not?

Approximately one year later I learned he had stayed and was very happy. With unusual enthusiasm she told of a change for the better in this boy. Next year a younger son would be enrolled in our elementary school.

How many souls' destinies were hanging upon my decision between heeding first and second thoughts that afternoon, I may never know. Oh, no! I hadn't intended to use any bad language. I wasn't even angry—only irritated and impatient. But had I given utterance to my feelings, it might have been just enough to sever a tie with the church which I did not even realize existed.

A LIFETIME'S REPENTANCE

In the judgment how many times over will we wish we had heeded the counsel with which we opened this chapter: "If thou hast thought evil, lay thine hand upon thy mouth." "A moment's petulance, a single gruff answer, a lack of Christian politeness and courtesy in some small matter, may result in the loss of both friends and influence."[5] "In one moment, by the hasty, passionate, careless tongue, may be wrought evil that a whole lifetime's repentance cannot undo. Oh, the hearts that are broken, the friends estranged, the lives wrecked, by the harsh, hasty words of those who might have brought help and healing!"[6]

Two mothers, though next-door neighbors and once good friends, had hardly spoken for twenty years because of one mother's hasty words over a childish prank.

Husbands have learned that apologies seldom, if ever, erase the effects of impetuous outbursts.

How many a mother's heart has been wounded by disrespectful words spoken by children who love her, but are among those who speak one moment before they think.

Abraham Lincoln wrote in a message to be read in Congress, December, 1862, "In times like the present men should utter nothing for which they would not willingly be responsible through time and eternity." If statesmen needed this counsel in 1862, surely we who are ambassadors of the King, and "upon whom the ends of the world are come,"[7] need it even more!

Tyron Edwards said, "Words are both better and worse than thoughts; they express them, and add to them; they give them power for good or evil; they start them on an endless flight, for instruction and comfort and blessing, or for injury and sorrow and ruin."

Will Carleton has expressed it well in this poem:

Boys flying kites haul in their white-winged birds;

You can't do that way when you're flying words. ... .

Thoughts unexpressed may sometimes fall back dead;

But God himself can't kill them once they're said.

Key **THINK TWICE BEFORE YOU SPEAK.**

CHANGE THAT TONE

"Let your light shine forth in pleasant words, in soothing tones of voice. Take all the sting out of them by prayer to God for self-control."[1]

F. R. Millard once referred to a French scientist's claim to have developed a stingless bee. He then quoted someone as saying, "Now he should go to work on men, and develop a stingless man!"

How often have you made a rather final decision either for or against a company's wares or services merely on the strength of the receptionist's tone of voice? How pleasant to use the telephone when the answerer has a smile in her voice!

An infant can be induced to laugh or cry merely by the tone of voice. Wild animals have been held at bay by soothing words calmly uttered. A dog's ears and tail will drop when even good words are harshly spoken.

A field publishing secretary in Africa once kindly told me, "Pastor, we need rebuke and correction at times, but don't be angry when you speak; have tears in your voice like Christ did." He referred to the following statement: "Christ Himself did not suppress one word of truth, but He spoke it always in love. He exercised the greatest tact, and thoughtful, kind attention in His intercourse with the people. He was never rude, never needlessly spoke a severe word, never gave needless pain to a sensitive soul. He did not censure human weakness. He fearlessly denounced hypocrisy, unbelief, and iniquity, but *tears were in His voice* as He uttered His scathing rebukes."[2]

Ellen White cautions us against attempting to reprove even with the same *words* which Christ used. Listen to the reasons why: "Christ sometimes reproved with severity, and in some cases it may be necessary for us to do so; but we should consider that while Christ knew the exact condition of the ones He rebuked, and just the amount of reproof they could bear, and what was necessary to correct their course of wrong, He also knew just how to pity the erring, comfort the unfortunate, and encourage the weak. He knew just how to keep souls from despondency and to inspire them with hope, because He was acquainted with the exact motives and peculiar trials of every mind. He could not make a mistake."[3]

PLEASURE IN IRRITATING

Are you sometimes tempted to believe that some people enjoy saying things in a sarcastic, cutting way—that they take pleasure in hurting others with their words? As inconceivable as this may seem, you may be right. "Some who profess to be servants of Christ have so long cherished the demon of unkindness that they seem to love the unhallowed element and to *take pleasure in speaking words that displease and irritate.* These men must be converted before Christ will acknowledge them as His children."[4]

While we must speak the truth, let's speak it in such a way as to make friends, insofar as possible, and not enemies. Take all of the "sting" out of your words. "Let your speech be always with grace, seasoned with salt,"[5] not with pepper or curry. Salt, wonderful salt— that which makes the flavor, or tone, just right, not flat or meaningless, nor hot and stinging.

| Key | *BE CAREFUL OF THE WAY YOU SPEAK.* |

TRY SMILING

A survey was made among 12,000 shoppers to discover why they preferred certain shops. Most liked low prices, but smiling clerks rated even more highly. Whose heart does not warm in the presence of a sincere smile! What would happen if everyone smiled only a little more?

The saying, "Smile and the world smiles with you," was never more true.

SMILE

Have you tried out your smile today
To light your steps along the way?
It's mirrored in each face you meet
On byway, path and city street.

Have you tried out your smile today—
A smile that's sunny, bright, and gay—
That helps to lift somebody's grief,
And brings to pain some small relief?

Have you tried out your smile today?
If not, you should, without delay.
You'll find your heart is gladdened too,
When someone else smiles back at you.[1]

EASIER TO SMILE

Some of us think we smile but often manage nothing more than a weak grin. It takes fifty-eight fewer muscles to smile than to frown, but just try smiling big at everyone you meet for one full day and see if your fourteen "smile muscles" aren't literally sore by evening. I've tried it and know that it's possible to smile until it hurts! But "smile soreness" will soon disappear if you keep up the smiling habit—and so will the suspicions of your friends that you "have something up your sleeve."

There may be times when smiles are inappropriate, but these occasions are few indeed. Seldom is anyone accused of smiling too much, but the name "sourpuss" is often heard.

"Look pleasant, please. As soon as I snap this picture you can resume your natural expression." This photographer's insinuation probably has most of us summed up about right.

SMILEY

H. P. Godwin tells the story of visiting his hometown after forty years' absence. He saw a modern department store over which flashed in neon the name "Smiley's." It brought to mind a lad of forty years before, the child of poverty-stricken parents, who lived on the "wrong side of town." From all outward appearances it seemed doubtful that he would ever make much of a mark in the world. But he had in his possession one priceless jewel—a sunny smile, and a desire to help others without thought of reward. This had earned for him the name "Smiley." Though it was hard to believe, this prosperous-looking store belonged to little Smiley. His smile, born of genuine goodness, had seen him through many a hard time, including the depression of the early thirties. As someone said in referring to this lad's climb to success, "You can't spray perfume around without getting some on yourself!"

TRY IT

Frowns won't get you anywhere;
    Try smiling.
When your face is lined with care,
    Try smiling.
When your goal seems far away,
And the world seems cold and gray,
It will help to smooth the way—
    Just smiling.[2]

Pastor J. N. Hunt, at a literature evangelists' institute, quoted Pastor Adlai Esteb as saying, "A smile is the light that illuminates the face and the fire that warms the heart." Both the quoter and the quoted named above knew how to smile and were successful in getting along with people. If you want to be successful, do what successful people do. To smile is not the least important.

If you don't like the faces of the people you meet, try changing them by changing your own. It could be that their faces are merely reflecting your expression. You can actually create the kind of people whom you like to meet! Try it. Literature evangelists, salespeople, and many others do it every day.

THE UNIVERSAL LANGUAGE

As one leaves the country of his birth, he soon discovers that language can be a real barrier between men. So we have found men through the years setting about to invent a universal language. One clever man devised a language called Esperanto. This language, purported to be easy for most everyone to learn, is designed to greatly reduce the problem of language barriers.

In South Africa there is a language called Fanegelo which if learned is supposed to make it possible for the European to communicate successfully with the African without either one having to learn the pure language of the other.

There is one language which appears to me to be truly universal-the language of the smile. Here there is no lengthy vocabulary list to memorize, no guttural sounds or "clicks" to master, no changes necessary from country to country or from tribe to tribe. All seem to understand this language without tutoring. You are introduced to someone as a "Christian." You want to tell him what this means. You want to say, "I like you. I want to be your friend. God loves you. There's something better ahead. I want to meet you in God's kingdom." But he speaks and understands only Sotho, and besides English you boast a vocabulary of 500 words in Zulu, which you have difficulty arranging in intelligible order. So what do you do?

You smile and grip the hand. Does he understand? Of course. How do you know he understands? He tells you—with a smile. He seems to say, "Yes. Thank you. I'll be there!"

When I was a student canvasser I was confronted with a woman almost past the "happy stage" of drunkenness. As she looked at me and my book through eyes that had lost the sparkle which liquor is supposed to give, I had the strong impression that my words weren't getting through. But I continued to smile. Presently she said to her husband, who was in a similar condition, "Ain't he got purdy teeth?" Then turning to me she said, "You shure are purdy." I was embarrassed, but she bought *Drama of the Ages*. Even in a near stupor she understood this language of the smile.

TOOTHLESS SMILE BETTER THAN NONE

In the county hospital in San Bernardino, California, there were two men who, because of paralysis, could speak only very poorly, but the moment I stepped into their ward they said, with this wonderful inaudible language, "I'm very happy to see you. I'm so glad you came. There's no one I'd rather see come through that door than you." And one of them hadn't a single tooth to boast of, and the other, whom they called "Sunshine," had but few, and in anything but attractive condition. But what beautiful smiles they had. What a pity that some of us fail to use this powerful means of communication simply because of a small gap between our two front teeth!

JESUS SMILES

I once knew a literature evangelist who was afraid of anything much more than a "rubber band" smile for fear of misrepresenting Christ. While it may be true that there is no place for vulgar boisterousness, "there are many who have an erroneous idea of the life and character of Christ. They think that He was devoid of warmth and sunniness, that He was stern, severe, and joyless. In many cases the whole religious experience is colored by these gloomy views.

"Our Saviour was deeply serious and intensely in earnest,

but never gloomy or morose. . . . The *religion of Jesus* gives peace like a river. It does not quench the light of joy; it *does not restrain cheerfulness nor cloud the sunny, smiling face."* [3] "Children [and others too!] hate the gloom of clouds and sadness. Their hearts respond to brightness, to cheerfulness, to love. . . . Smile, parents; smile teachers. If your heart is sad, let not your face reveal the fact."[4]

Your *words* may not always reach the mind of the one whom you try to help, but you know the "universal language." It reaches every heart. Speak it often!

 **Key** **SMILE.**

BE HUMBLE

"I think I could be a great preacher if it weren't for this message!" declared D. M. Canright to a friend just after leaving the pulpit one day. Not long after this he became an avowed enemy of the Seventh-day Adventist Church. He died years later a broken man, feeling it was too late to come back.

"Pride goeth before destruction, and an haughty spirit before a fall. Better it is to be of an humble spirit with the lowly, than to divide the spoil with the proud."[1]

"Praising yourself to the sky will not get you there," an unknown wise man once said. "Every man who praises himself brushes the luster from his best efforts."[2]

BLOWING YOUR OWN HORN

Self-praise seldom gets you anywhere in this world and certainly is not a heavenly characteristic. Ellen G. White tells us, "Those who are self-confident, and think their way is above criticism, will show very imperfect work."[3]

It is better to think less of yourself than others think of you. "The best way to make sure that any big shot is really big is to observe that he never acts Mr. Big at all."[4]

"Those who feel great may be lightly esteemed of God because of the perversity of their hearts. Our only safety is to lie low at the foot of the cross, be little in our own eyes, and trust in God; for He alone can make us great."[5]

"'Before honor is humility.'[6] To fill a high place before men, Heaven chooses the worker who, like John the Baptist, takes a lowly place before God. The most childlike disciple is the most efficient in labor for God. The heavenly intelligence's can cooperate with him who is seeking, not to exalt self, but to save souls. He who feels most deeply his need of divine aid will plead for it; and the Holy Spirit will give unto him glimpses of Jesus that will strengthen and uplift the soul.

From communion with Christ he will go forth to work for those who are perishing in their sins. He is anointed for his mission; and he succeeds where many of the learned and intellectually wise would fail."[7]

HUMILITY BETTER THAN RICHES

Former Prime Minister Macmillan concluded an address at Liverpool with these words: "Throughout our country we need a rekindling of faith in Divine Providence, which has sustained and inspired our people through this long and often hazardous journey in British history. The world today is rich—perhaps too rich—in technical and scientific knowledge. Only true, *humble faith* can give mankind the wisdom to do right."

If the prosperity of an earthly kingdom is dependent upon humble faith rather than upon trust in riches and knowledge, surely the church cannot advance unless her members seek an abundant supply of this precious commodity called humility.

"When men exalt themselves, feeling that they are a necessity for the success of God's great plan, the Lord causes them to be set aside. It is made evident that the Lord is not dependent upon them. The work does not stop because of their removal from it, but goes forward with greater power."[8]

LET OTHERS SAY IT

A singer once told me he sang "beautifully," and a speaker referred to his own thoughts as "wonderful." The singing was beautiful and the thoughts were wonderful, but it would have been more becoming to let others do the judging.

If you are wise and capable, others will discover it and pass the word along. And when the word does get back to you, see that you never pass it on. "We are to use every power of our being in His service, and after we have done our utmost, we are still to regard ourselves as unprofitable servants."[9]

Humility is a rare trait of character which will prove an otherwise well-informed man to be truly wise. It will cause one not only to receive suggestions, correction, and rebuke *gracefully,* but to be truly *grateful* for advice and the pointing out of mistakes and weaknesses.

"Solomon was never so rich or so wise or so truly great as when he confessed, 'I am but a little child: I know not how to go out or come in.'"[10]

Key | **BE HUMBLE.**

WHEN OTHERS DON'T SEE THINGS YOUR WAY

There have been states and countries which have always been on the winning side. They watched the greater powers carefully to discover who was winning and then, though remaining somewhat neutral, leaned toward that power. One country, during World War II, changed her military dress and style of marching to match somewhat the forces which had now become apparently stronger. Earlier another country, then "winning," had been the model for this "neutral" country's army. We read that people living in certain of the states during the Civil War owned both Yankee and Confederate flags. Which one was displayed was determined by which army was nearest.

JOIN THEM

Attitudes which are behind actions such as these have brought forth the saying, "If you can't lick them, join them!" If your opponents are winning, some would say, join them and you too will be a winner. In wartime this attitude would no doubt be branded by many as sheer cowardice, though even in war it is not always easy to discover whose cause is the most "right." Seldom are the issues entirely clear-cut, except in the minds of those who are victims of one-sided propaganda.

In dealing with issues other than political or military, there may also be more than one right way. Though we may think our way the best, how much more would be accomplished if at times we adapted our methods to fit another's way of thinking! Often there is no real principle at stake, but just a preference in method. How much better to "join" the one who seems to oppose your ideas, and work together with him toward accomplishing a common end! To "go it alone" or not at all just because you are set in your ways will seldom help you reach your goal.

BE ADAPTABLE

Does the end justify the means? We could hardly subscribe to this, but we surely must admit there is often more than one legitimate way to accomplish the same good thing. After all, there is nothing in the Bible, or even international law, to give us guidance as to the rightness or wrongness of many preferences of nations, tribes, or persons.

We have all noticed the footpaths cutting across public parks or college campuses. Were there not enough sidewalks? "Keep off the grass" signs were numerous, but still the marred lawns. Wise were the university administrators who, instead of posting signs to force students to use the "right" path, planted the grass first and later built the sidewalks where the footpaths had appeared!

Yes, "if you can't lick them, join them," unless there is some principle at stake. And if you think there is a principle involved, make sure it is of the heavenly kind and not one of your own making before you dedicate to it all your defensive powers .

UNITY IN DIVERSITY

"The religion of Christ does not require us to lose our identity of character, but merely to adapt ourselves, in some measure, to the feelings and ways of others. Many people may be brought together in a unity of religious faith whose opinions, habits, and tastes in temporal matters are not in harmony; but if they have the love of Christ glowing in their bosoms, and are looking forward to the same heaven as their eternal home, they may have the sweetest and most intelligent communion together, and a unity the most wonderful."[1]

"Some . . . are inclined to indulge the spirit manifested by the apostle John when he said: 'Master, we saw one casting out devils in Thy name; and we forbade him, because he followeth not with us.'. . If their life and character are exemplary, let all work who will, in any capacity. Although they may not conform exactly to your methods, not a word should be spoken to condemn or discourage them."[2]

Let us never become too fond of our own opinions, ideas, and methods. Rather adopt the principle of the apostle Paul, who was "made all things to all men" that he "might by all means save some."[3]

Be firm to true principles, but make allowances for those who see things differently.

| Key | BE UNOPINIONATED AND ADAPTABLE. |

IF I COULD JUST GET ORGANIZED

Every day people lose jobs, miss promotions, get even subordinates down on them, and experience serious marital difficulties because of disorganized living.

Our irregularity may have more to do with our "people problems" than we realize. Even your milkman of yesteryear may have come to dislike the very sight of your house because you had no bottles out one day and so many he couldn't carry them the next, in addition to changing your order every other day.

Children like a good amount of order too, and so does most everyone else. It's interesting how upset even the chronically disorganized man becomes when the undisciplined habits of others cause him trouble.

PEOPLE MORE DIFFICULT THAN DOGS

Dogs like their bone at somewhere near the same time every day, though they don't usually grumble and complain much. They just "grin 'n' bear it." But don't expect the same of people. Remember that dogs are easier to get along with than people! Husbands and children will growl more than Fido when supper is two hours late.

Does the following poem describe your life?

IF I COULD JUST GET ORGANIZED

There may be nothing wrong with you,

The way you live, the work you do,

But I can very plainly see

Exactly what is wrong with me.

It isn't that I'm indolent

Or dodging duty by intent;
I work as hard as anyone,
And yet I get so little done.
The morning goes, the noon is here;
Before I know, the night is near;
And all around me, I regret,
Are things I haven't finished yet.
If I could just get organized!
I oftentimes have realized
Not all that matters is the man;
The man must also have a plan.
With you, there may be nothing wrong;
But here's my trouble right along:
I do the things that don't amount
To very much, of no account,
That really seem important though,
And let a lot of matters go.
I nibble this, I nibble that,
But never finish what I'm at.
I work as hard as anyone,
And yet, I get so little done.
I'd do so much you'd be surprised,
If I could just get organized![1]

SATAN'S WAY TO WEAKEN CHURCH

Amusing though it may at times seem, disorganization is not a laughing matter.

"If we see no necessity for harmonious action, and are disorderly, undisciplined, and disorganized in our course of action, angels, who are thoroughly organized and move in perfect order, cannot work for us successfully. They turn away in grief, for they are not authorized to bless confusion, distraction, and disorganization. All who desire the cooperation of the heavenly messengers must work in unison with them. Those who have the unction from on high will in all their efforts encourage order, discipline, and union of action, and then the angels of God can cooperate with them. But never, never will these heavenly messengers place their endorsement upon irregularity, disorganization, and disorder."[2]

"It is a sin to be heedless, purposeless, and indifferent in any work in which we may engage, but especially in the work of God. Every enterprise connected with His cause should be carried forward with order, forethought, and earnest prayer."[3] "Order is heaven's first law."[4] Does that surprise you? Order before love? Can even love, at least in this world, apart from her "twin sister . . .duty," produce good results?[5] Love without God-given definition and direction is meaningless at best and destructive at worst.

FIVE MINUTES LATE

Does this exclamation by an eighteenth-century author, Hannah Cowley, echo your own despair? "I have been five minutes too late all my lifetime!" Don't give up. You can change. God bids us, "Never be late to an appointment,"[6] and "all His biddings are enablings."[7]

Only those who have had the always-late habit can appreciate how difficult it is to overcome. But surely it cannot be impossible to be always five minutes *early* instead of five minutes late. One successful American businessman said, "I owe my success in life to being always fifteen minutes ahead of time." That this matter of promptness is usually only a problem of decision, discipline and habit is evidenced by the fact that the five-minute-late person is no more than five minutes late whether the appointed time be 9:00 or 9:30!

"Persons who have not acquired habits of close industry and economy of time, should have set rules to prompt them to regularity and dispatch."[8] "Men of business can be truly successful only by having regular hours for rising, for prayer, for meals, and for retiring. If order and regularity are essential in worldly business, how much more so in the work of God!"[9]

THE NOTEBOOK HABIT

I am repeatedly amazed at the very practical counsel the spirit of prophecy gives on almost every phase and problem of living. Many, if not most, successful people find that heeding the following counsel greatly increases their productivity and happiness, whether preacher or housewife, literature evangelist or office secretary. "When you rise in the morning, take into consideration, as far as possible, the work you must accomplish during the day. If necessary, have a small book in which to jot down the things that need to be done, and set yourself a time in which to do your work."[10]

I once heard R. H. Pierson say, "A short pencil is better than a long memory." How true!

If you want more peace of mind, a happier homelife, more success at your work, more contented children, the help of heavenly angels and fewer regrets, live an orderly life.

| Key | *GET ORGANIZED.* |

LOOK YOUR BEST

Some Christians have been satisfied that they have completed their "dress reform" when they have culled from their wardrobe, jewel chest and cosmetics cabinet all those things which they should not wear. But however important the "shouldn'ts" may be, let's look at some of the "shoulds."

MULTIPLY YOUR INFLUENCE

"The influence of believers would be tenfold greater if men and women who accept the truth, who have been formerly careless and slack in their habits, would be so elevated and sanctified through the truth as to observe habits of *neatness, order,* and *good taste* in their dress."[1]

Is the sister who says, "I don't care how my hair looks," giving evidence of humility, or of laziness and unconcern for the glory of God's name? Face lifts may be optional, but could it be that those of us who are careless of our appearance need "soul-lifts"?

GOOD TASTE NOT PRIDE

I have heard it said, when referring to excess makeup, extreme hairdos, much jewelry, and immodest attire: "You can tell what's on the inside by what you see on the outside." But does not the opposite extreme also give evidence of disorder within? Referring to those who dress without "order and taste" and who "class decency and neatness with pride," an inspired pen says, "Those who are careless and untidy in dress are seldom elevated in their conversation and possess but little refinement of feeling."[2]

SOULS LOST BY POOR DRESS

"The loss of some souls at last will be traced to the untidiness of the minister. . . . Some who minister in sacred things so arrange their dress upon their persons, that, to some extent at least, it destroys the influence of their labor. There is an apparent *lack of taste in color and neatness of fit.*"[3]

Could it really be that souls will be lost because of our lack of regard for appropriate color and color combinations? Is our great Creator concerned with the "neatness of fit," the tailoring of our clothing? Our dress should have "grace" and " natural beauty,"[4] we are told. "We should seek to make the best of our appearance"[5] by being neither "overdressed" nor "by dressing in a lax, untidy manner."[6] There appears to be neither pride nor hypocrisy in putting one's best foot forward.

And what well-balanced counsel is this! "Furnish them [your children] with becoming garments, that they may not be mortified by their appearance, for this would be injurious to their self-respect. . . . It is always right to be neat and to be clad appropriately, in a manner becoming to your age and station in life."[7]

Our heavenly Father even cares about our self-respect! A Christian schoolgirl needn't dress like a grandmother, nor should a Christian grandmother dress like a teenager! And He urges that "station in life"—profession or occupation—be taken into consideration in determining appropriate dress.

If you want to have tenfold greater influence for good, and want more self-respect and greater respect from wife, husband, children, and colleagues, take pains to be attractive and appropriate for each situation and opportunity.

Key | **MAKE THE BEST OF YOUR APPEARANCE.**

TO BE YOUNG

Never look down on youthfulness, either in others or in yourself.

K. H. Wood reminds us: "Many great exploits of history were accomplished by young people. Alexander of Greece conquered the world at thirty-three. Sir Isaac Newton discovered the law of gravitation at twenty-three. Joan of Arc achieved fame and was burned at the stake at nineteen. Lindbergh flew the Atlantic at twenty-five.

"Young people have also been in the forefront of many religious advances. Martin Luther posted the theses that gave impetus to the German Reformation when he was thirty-four. John Calvin added the force of his life to the cause of the Reformation at nineteen. Roger Williams was a banished heretic at thirty-two. James White was preaching at twenty-one; and in six weeks 1,000 souls were converted. J. N. Loughborough began preaching the advent message at twenty. Ellen Harmon was chosen as God's special messenger when she was but seventeen."[1]

A FATAL MISCALCULATION

"Adults sometimes express lack of confidence in youth because they assume that youth are unprepared to meet the hard realities of life. This attitude toward youth is not new. About 3,000 years ago King Saul tried to prevent young David from even trying to fight Goliath. Note his small confidence in youth. He said, 'Thou art not able to go against this Philistine to fight with him: for thou art but a youth, and he a man of war from his youth.' 1 Samuel 17:33.

"Goliath scoffed at youth's ability to fight him. 'When the Philistine looked about, and saw David, he disdained him: for he was but a youth.' Verse 42. Goliath's defiance of Israel seemed to reach its peak in his expression of absolute disdain for youthful David. But his miscalculation concerning David was a fatal error. It caused him foolishly, in utter contempt and defiance, to push back his helmet. Goliath apparently believed that of necessity all youth must be handicapped by inexperience. How wrong he was!"[2]

"Top management of gigantic industrial enterprises are searching as never before for men and women who possess that God-given magic touch in human relations, enabling them to move ahead rapidly in the realm of management, and become executives and administrators of proven stability and wisdom *at an earlier age then ever before.*"[3]

If you are older, never be guilty of looking with disdain upon a man's ideas and efforts simply because he is young in years.

A GOOD RECIPE

On the other hand, the young worker must not demand the respect of his elders—he must earn it. If you feel that you are mistreated, the fault may be in your attitudes and have nothing to do with your years. The counsel to young Timothy is not to be used as a weapon for demanding respect, but as a recipe for earning it. Hear 1 Timothy 4:12 as Dr. Phillips translates it: "Don't let people look down on you because you are young; see that they look up to you because you are an example to them in your speech and behavior, in your love and faith and sincerity."

And remember, the truly wise youth, even with impressive educational certificates and degrees, will never think himself so wise that he cannot learn. He will ever be a willing, eager learner.

REBUKE A WISE MAN

"Rebuke a wise man, and he will love thee. Give instruction to a wise man, and he will be yet wiser: teach a just man, and he will increase in learning."[4] "He who will not learn of anyone except himself, has a fool for a teacher."[5] "No one ever begins to become 'somebody' until he has learned to respect those who have already become 'somebody.'"[6] Good "followership" will always precede good leadership.

It is little wonder that a certain young worker had difficulties when he expressed a dislike for working under men with education inferior to his own. He still needed to learn that true education and wisdom are not always measured by the number of years a man spends at school.

"If you act like a child, then you must expect to be treated like a child," said Gervais to his son who complained that his views were so often ignored in family affairs.

If you are not young, don't look down on those who are. If you are young, see that you *earn* the respect of those who are older. It is neither right nor necessary that youthfulness be despised.

Key | ***VALUE PEOPLE BY ABILITY, NOT AGE***

COURAGE TO BE WRONG

After being punished by his mother for throwing stones at his playmate, my four-year-old son prayed thus at worship time: "Help Mamma not to be so cruel to me, and help Henry not to be so naughty so I won't have to throw stones at him anymore."

Unfortunately, this spirit of self-justification is not limited to little children and becomes less laughable when manifested by those of us who are older. How hard it is for most of us to admit our wrongs. How little we understand about confessing our faults one to another. Often our confessions go something like this: "I'm sorry I spoke as I did, but you make me *so* angry." Have you noticed that our so-called confessions place the blame on the other person for our wrongs?

THE CHIEF OFFENDER

God's servant gives us a formula for confession that will humble most of us: "If you have committed one wrong and they twenty, confess that one as though you were the chief offender."[1] Analyze your confessions critically and see if you don't often make the other person, or circumstances, the "chief offender" rather than yourself.

How much we hurt ourselves by being so full of excuses. "Of all human inventions, we believe the most worthless is an excuse,"[2] said someone. It's a sign of strength, not weakness, to say, "I'm sorry. I was wrong. Please forgive me." Why not be a little hard on ourselves and give the other person the benefit of the doubt rather than reluctantly saying, "Well-l-l, I suppose I *may* have been wrong in getting angry, but—" "The religion of Christ will lead us to be kind and courteous and not so tenacious of our opinions. We should die to self and esteem others better than ourselves."[3]

"If pride and selfishness were laid aside, five minutes would remove most difficulties. Angels have been grieved and God displeased by the hours which have been spent in justifying self."[4]

CUSTOMER ALWAYS WRONG

Some of us are like the policeman who, when asked how he liked his job, said, "The pay isn't too high, the hours are long, and you walk in all kinds of weather—but the part I really like is, the customer is always wrong."[5]

Most everyone is skilled in the art of twisting facts in such a way that he is never really wrong. When an American runner beat a Russian in a track event in which only the two of them participated, the sports writer for the Russian paper did not know how to report the result without admitting the Russian defeat. His editor had had more experience. He simply wrote: "Ivan came in second, but the American was next to last."[6]

Pastor D. M. Malotle, youth leader in South Africa, told the story of a man who climbed a tree and left his wife and child alone to face a hungry lion. When questioned about his cowardice his excuse was ready: "When I get angry I don't know what I'm doing, so when I saw that lion near my child I became so angry that I just climbed the tree!"

WE MADE A MISTAKE

"A good leader takes a little more than his share of blame; a little less than his share of credit."[7] I once worked as a carpenter under a foreman who practiced this. When those under him made a mistake, even though costly, he would tell the "big boss," "We made a mistake." And when he was in any way responsible for the mistake, he would say, "I made a mistake."

Let us beware lest we fall into the same category as does the type of minister described by Pastor E. E. Cleveland: "Occasionally one meets a minister who doesn't trust anything or anyone but himself. To him, leadership is a curse when he is not leading. And dissent is more than a privilege; it is an obligation. From his point of view all agreement is politics, and unity is a sign of Laodicean apathy. He thrives on controversy and is at his best while dissecting the 'brethren.' In his eyes the church can do no right and he no wrong. He would save all that the church spends and spend all that it saves. And what is more, he would spend with different people and for different things."[8]

Our almost incurable tendency toward being opinionated may be summed up in this bit of introspection: "We never harbor ill feelings against individuals who disagree with our views, although we often regret that so many people can be wrong!"[9]

It's good to be well informed, but you'll get along better with people if you're not afraid to say occasionally, "I don't know." You ask directions. How much do you think of the person who hesitates to say "I don't know," and sends you miles out of your way? A teacher many years ago asked his students in turn, "What is electricity?" Several cautiously replied, "I don't know." One student said, "I did know, but I've forgotten." The teacher exclaimed, "What a loss to science! The only man who ever knew, and he's forgotten!" It's best to know, but if you don't, admit it.

Some of us should pray daily that God will help us learn to take correction and advice gracefully—and even gratefully. When the great David, conscious that he was destined to be the king of the nation, was rebuked by the humble farmer's wife, Abigail, he said with repentance and gratitude, "Blessed be the Lord God of Israel, which sent thee this day to meet me: and blessed be thy advice, and blessed be thou, which hast kept me this day from coming to shed blood, and from avenging myself with mine own hand."[10] "There are many who, when they are reproved, think it praiseworthy if they receive the rebuke without becoming impatient; but how few take reproof with gratitude of heart and bless those who seek to save them from pursuing an evil course."[11]

Key | **WHEN YOU'RE WRONG, ADMIT IT.**

PLAYING FAVORITES

Elder C. L. Paddock writes of a conductor who shouted rudely at a lame man in work clothing trying to board the train. "Come on, old man, hurry up! We can't keep this train waiting all day," he said.

Later, when he was collecting the tickets, a passenger asked him, "Do you know who that old gentleman is?"

"No, I don't know who he is, and I don't care, either," was the reply. But when he learned that the lame man was the president of the railroad, he hastened to make apologies, explaining, "I thought you were just one of our customers."

"It doesn't matter who I am," said the old gentleman. "If you had been rude to anyone who paid a fare to ride this train, I would ask that you be taken from your job. You saw I was lame and needed help. You should have offered to help me instead of abusing me."[1]

Is *our* conduct toward others frequently determined more by *who* they are than by their need? Let's read on, examining ourselves all the while, and find out.

President McKinley is known on at least one occasion to have given his seat on the streetcar to a poor washerwoman while others remained seated.[2] Would we have done the same?

A SACK OF POTATOES

Awaiting supper after a busy Sabbath, I decided to get some exercise walking up a hill opposite my hotel. I had not gone far before I found myself overtaking an African woman struggling up the hill with a baby on her back and a large bag of potatoes on her head. No doubt she had been sent to the store for potatoes after a hard day's work. I was sure she was not in need of exercise, as I was. Momentarily I hesitated. What would others think if I carried those potatoes for her? Then I asked myself, "What would Jesus do?" I thought of my own mother—at one time she had done housework for others to help us children remain in church school.

"May I help you?" I offered. She glanced at me in surprise. A faint smile of appreciation lighted her face. "Yes, thank you," she replied hesitantly.

I am not sure just what people thought as they saw a well dressed young man carrying a sack of potatoes up the hill for an African servant. But I believe Jesus would have done the same—only with *no* thoughts of self, even momentarily.

You and I will continue to have people problems as long as we are concerned only with those who can return our favors.

THE GOOD SAMARITAN

Commenting on Jesus' story of the Good Samaritan, E. G. White says: "He showed that our neighbor does not mean merely one of the church or faith to which we belong. It has no reference to race, color, or class distinction. Our neighbor is every person who needs our help."[3]

"He's a wonderful man!" said a little girl of Pastor J. D. Harcombe after he had visited in her home.

"Why do you say, 'He's a wonderful man'?" her father asked.

"Why, Daddy, he even saw *me* in the room!"

Let us also see everyone in the room, the young and old, those "above" and "beneath," those of all races and stations, those who need help as well as those who can help us.

The mother of several sons, including the famous World War II hero, General Douglas MacArthur, was once asked, at a time of special honor for Douglas, "Aren't you proud of your son?"

"Which one?" she replied with classic impartiality.

Are we sometimes partial in out attitudes toward our children, our church members, our fellow workers?

A FAKE

A young boy walked through the streets of Paris with his grandfather. As a beggar approached, Grandfather gave the boy some coins to hand to him. Grandfather later reproved the boy for not tipping his hat as he placed the coins in the beggar's hands.

"Why should I?" asked the lad. "The beggar was blind."

"Ah," Grandfather said, "how do you know? He may have been a fake."

"Christianity will make a man a gentleman"[4] even in the presence of a pretender.

SAVING AN ENEMY

During the American Revolution there lived in Pennsylvania a faithful minister of the gospel named Peter Miller. Near him lived a man who was violently opposed to him and who openly abused him and his followers. This man was found guilty of treason and was sentenced to death.

No sooner was the sentence pronounced than Miller set out on foot to see General Washington to intercede for the man's life. He was told that the petition for his friend could not be granted.

"My *friend!* He is not my friend," answered Miller. "I have not a worse enemy living than that man."

"What?" asked Washington. "You have walked sixty miles to save the life of your enemy? That in my judgment puts the matter in an entirely different light. I will grant the pardon."

The pardon was made out, and Miller at once began walking to the place of execution. He arrived just as the man was being taken to the scaffold. The traitor, on seeing Miller in the crowd, exclaimed, "Why, there is old Peter Miller. He has come all the way from Ephrata to have his revenge gratified today by seeing me hanged!"

These words were scarcely spoken when Miller stepped

forward and produced the pardon. The life of his worst enemy was spared.

Have we not here a picture of God? "When we were enemies, we were reconciled to God by the death of His Son."[5]

TRUE CHRISTIAN LOVE

True Christian love will embrace even those who intentionally, or unintentionally, cause us anguish and suffering. We refer with a bit of justified irony to Job's comforters. But, "the Lord turned the captivity of Job" when he prayed for these friends. He was blessed when he dropped his holier-than-thou attitude and was no longer "righteous in his own eyes."[6]

Christian human relations plays no favorites. Let us learn the lesson of true Christian love.

| Key | *BE NOT A RESPECTER OF PERSONS.* |

SOUR STOMACHS
AND WORDS

The day at the office had been more difficult than usual. You tried to persuade yourself that six hours sleep the night before would be sufficient. You felt hungry as you finished that last chapter at about 11:45, so you had some cookies (not more than three or four, or was it six?) and a glass of milk. Sleep came quickly, but so did morning. An extra "wink" turned out to be half an hour, so off you went without breakfast. You didn't feel too hungry anyway. A doughnut at ten would do.

Now it's 6:45. You couldn't get home a minute earlier. Your stomach, though you really haven't eaten much today, is upset. "Those tablets just don't work!" you mutter. The sounds of happy children, your children, seem to pound against your eardrums. Three aspirin have not entirely freed your head from pain.

"People problems" even at home? You love your family, of course! But a man has to have someplace to "blow off steam" after a hard day's work, doesn't he? "Do I have to be at my best behavior even in my own home?" you wonder. "Perhaps she'd like to trade places with me for a day or two. Then she'd understand!" And so begins another "pleasant" evening. Why can't my home be that haven of rest I've read about?" you puzzle.

THIEF OF PATIENCE

"It is next to an impossibility for an intemperate person to be patient."[1]

Patience—that rare and beautiful trait of character which, when possessed, solves or prevents a good percentage of our "people problems." How sad, but true, that we so often allow intemperance to steal away our patience!

How can we expect even the dog to be happy to see us when

we're half sick and mad at the world because of our "overs" and "unders"—overwork, overeating, over reading, listening, and watching; under sleeping, under exercising, under playing, relaxing, and praying?

Don't we find ourselves apologizing too often for saying the wrong things, for grumbling and growling around the house? You inherited a bad disposition? Perhaps. But let's not forget that even some animals' natures can be well-nigh transformed merely by adjusting the quality and quantity of their food. Don't let the momentary pleasures of overeating, or any other form of intemperance, rob you of happy human relations.

SOUR STOMACHS AND CHURCH BOARDS

Does your temperance or intemperance have anything to do with the progress or hindrance of the work of the church?

"The effects of wrong eating are brought into council and board meetings. The brain is affected by the condition of the stomach. A disordered stomach is productive of a disordered, uncertain state of mind. A diseased stomach produces a diseased condition of the brain and often makes one obstinate in maintaining erroneous opinions. The supposed wisdom of such a one is foolishness with God.

"I present this as the cause of the situation in many council and board meetings, where questions demanding careful study have been given but little consideration, and decisions of the greatest importance have been hurriedly made. Often when there should have been unanimity of sentiment in the affirmative, decided negatives have entirely changed the atmosphere pervading a meeting. These results have been presented to me again and again.

"I present these matters now because I am instructed to say to my brethren in the ministry: By intemperance in eating you disqualify yourselves for seeing clearly the difference between sacred and common fire."[2]

Let us beware lest our thoughts and tongues be controlled by sour stomachs rather than by clear minds!

Key BE TEMPERATE.

SAY THANK YOU

The following little story is probably so oft retold because the ingratitude which created it is so oft repeated.

A rather queenly young woman boarded a crowded city bus. A tired little man got up and gave her his seat. There was a moment of silence.

"I beg your pardon?" said the tired little man.

"I didn't say anything," rejoined the young woman.

"I'm sorry," said the little man. "I thought you said 'Thank you.'"

Are we, who are old enough to know better, still like the little child who is often reminded by mother, "Say Thank you"?

How often have you entertained people in your home, sometimes total strangers, to ease the burden of their loneliness, without receiving a note of thanks? How many a weary wife, who has been forced to neglect her children and other duties and turn her home into a virtual hotel, could truly say of most of her guests, "I've never heard from them since"!

A BITTER STING

Though we do not do our good deeds for love of praise, even the saintly Joseph found ingratitude hard to bear. The king's cupbearer professed deep gratitude for the interpretation of his dream; but when he was released from prison, he forgot about Joseph's kindness to him. "For two years longer Joseph remained a prisoner. The hope that had been kindled in his heart gradually died out, and to all other trials was added *the bitter sting of ingratitude.*"[1]

The selfless Jesus "desires us to *appreciate* the great plan of redemption . . . and to walk before Him . . . with *grateful thanksgiving . . . He longs to see gratitude welling up in our hearts*

. . . To praise God in fullness and sincerity of heart is as much a duty as is prayer."[2]

During His agony in Gethsemane Jesus had "a yearning desire to hear some words of comfort" from His sleeping disciples. "if He could only know that His disciples understood and appreciated" the momentous decision He faced on their behalf, "He would be strengthened."[2] These drowsy three could have done the work of sinless angels in comforting and strengthening the Saviour at this hour, but the habit of ingratitude denied them this privilege.

Though flattery may be deceitful, do not ever conclude that expressions of genuine gratitude are wrong. If the human nature of our Lord received strength and comfort from expressions of gratitude and appreciation, surely we should not deny our struggling fellow travelers on the road to heaven this encouragement. Know the difference between flattery and genuine expressions of gratitude.

"We should be self-forgetful, ever looking out for opportunities, even in little things, to show gratitude for the favors we have received from others."[4]

INGRATITUDE A SIN

Have you and I been guilty of accepting the gifts, hospitality and kindness of others without feeling and expressing gratitude? Or is it important? Surely ingratitude is one of the prevailing sins of this age. Sin? Yes, sin—a problem of the soul. Jesus recognized ingratitude as symptomatic of soul poverty when He asked the one thankful leper, "Where are the nine?"[5]

I suppose we do at times express "gratitude" when we don't feel grateful simply because our mothers so often reminded us to say Thank you, but if we are not truly grateful—from the heart—for the kindness shown us by God and man, we will very often find ourselves among "the nine."

"Unless you cultivate a cheerful, happy, *grateful* frame of mind, Satan will eventually lead you captive at his will."[6] True gratitude is a gift from God, as are all other Christian graces.

Are you sorry for your unthankfulness? Confess it to God, and to wife or husband, or child or friend. Christ can then come into the life and make you habitually like the one who "turned back" "giving . . . thanks." [7]

Key *BE GRATEFUL.*

SPEAK NO EVIL

"Among some species of animals, if one of their number is wounded and falls, he is at once set upon and torn in pieces by his fellows. The same cruel spirit is indulged by men and women who bear the name of Christians. . . . There are some who point to other's faults and failures to divert attention from their own, or to gain credit for great zeal for God and the church."[1]

A young couple came into the church through the efforts of a literature evangelist. A church member felt it necessary to share with them facts proving that some of the local church leaders were far from perfect. They were shocked, and almost discouraged with their new-found faith.

A Bible study was in session in a Seventh-day Adventist home. Voices from the kitchen were overheard by the would-be converts. The sordid deeds of a fallen minister were being discussed. The Bible studies came to a sudden halt. How much harm is wrought by gossip, criticism, and evil speaking we'll doubtless never know!

SATAN'S SPECIAL TEMPTATION

Surely there must be some reason why so much has been written under inspiration warning us of the dangers of criticism and gossip. The reason is that the habit of dwelling upon and publishing the defects of others "is *Satan's special temptation,* whereby he strives to hinder the work."[2]

Let us not deceive ourselves into thinking criticism and gossip are not harmful if what we say is true. We congratulate ourselves that we speak only the straight truth and say nothing about a man behind his back which we wouldn't say to his face. This does not remove our guilt or the harm done.

"If sin is plain in a brother, breathe it not to another," [3] urges

God's servant. We are talking here about plain sins, real defects—nothing imaginary; but the counsel is, "breathe it not to another."

Prefixing our remarks with, "I suppose I shouldn't say this, but—" makes us none the more innocent. Even "when tempted" merely "to complain of what someone has said or done," we are urged rather to "praise something in that person's life or character."[4]

One of these complaints about something someone had said was made to me. My informant, and good friend, immediately realized his mistake and expressed his repentance: "I shouldn't have told you that. Here you thought he was such a good man, and I've prejudiced your mind against him." And so he had. His repentance was sincere and accepted, but too late. My esteem for the other man had been lowered.

PRAY

"We have not a moment to spend in criticism and accusation. Let those who have done this in the past fall on their knees in prayer."[5]

"All have sinned and come short." Is it therefore surprising that we could spend our whole life criticizing and possibly not tell a single lie? The very fact that we ourselves are so sinful and erring should cause us to feel like Dwight L. Moody, who said, "I have had so much trouble with myself that I never had time to find fault with the other fellow." In fact, most of our suspicions of others are aroused by what we know of ourselves. "If you insist on perfection, make the first demand on yourself."[6]

Someone has said, "There are two kinds of people: good and bad. The classifying is done by the good."[7] No, we don't often put ourselves in the "bad" category. But let us face the fact that we're all "bad" by nature—lost, depraved sinners, saved only by grace—in need of help more than of criticism, condemnation, and stoning. Jesus said, "He that is without sin among you, let him first cast a stone."[8]

PEOPLE IN YOUR MOUTH

How strange to think that a mind could become so twisted that it would actually enjoy dwelling upon the sins and defects of others! Yet the messenger of the Lord asserts that "there are many who find *special enjoyment* in discoursing and dwelling upon the defects, whether real or imaginary, of those who bear heavy responsibilities in connection with the institutions of God's cause." "These persons," she continues, "are spiritually dwarfed by continually dwelling upon the failings and faults of others. They are morally incapable of discerning good and noble actions, unselfish endeavors, true heroism, and self-sacrifice. . . . They are not cultivating that charity that should characterize the Christian's life. They are degenerating every day and are becoming narrower in their prejudices and views. Littleness is their element, and the atmosphere that surrounds them is poisonous to peace and happiness."[9]

There may yet be found some good religion in the words purportedly spoken by the old cannibal chief to his son: "Young man, don't talk while you have people in your mouth!" As long as our minds and mouths are full of bad things about people, we would be wise not to talk at all.

IGNORANCE CREATES CRITICISM

How much of our criticism and faultfinding is based on ignorance of the facts! When a lighthouse was being built on a dangerous shore in the frozen Northwest, a couple of Eskimos watched the whole proceeding suspiciously. After it was finished, a heavy fog rolled in one night, covering shore, lighthouse, and land. Said one Eskimo triumphantly to the other, "I told you white igloo builder no good. Light shine, bell ding-dong, horn woo-woo, but fog come rolling in just the same!"[10]

Of those who criticize the work of others, an inspired pen says, "Had they been left to do the work, they would either have refused to move at all under the attending discouragement's of the case, or would have managed more indiscreetly than those who did do the work."[11]

PREACHERS FOR DINNER

A Seventh-day Adventist father, when lamenting and wondering over the fact that his children had all left the church, was bluntly told by his close friend, "The reason your children left the church is because you ate the preacher for dinner every Sabbath!" "Let not the conversation in your homes be poisoned with criticism of the Lord's workers. Parents who indulge this criticizing spirit are not bringing before their children that which will make them wise unto salvation. Their words tend to unsettle the faith and confidence not only of the children, but of those older in years."[12] And "no Christian parent should permit gossip to be repeated in the family circle or remarks to be made disparaging the members of the church."[13]

NO CRITICS IN HEAVEN

"I saw that some are withering spiritually. They have lived some time watching to keep their brethren straight—watching for every fault to make trouble with them. And while doing this, their minds are not on God, nor on heaven, nor on the truth; but just where Satan wants them—on someone else. Their souls are neglected; they seldom see or feel their own faults, for they have had enough to do to watch the faults of others without so much as looking to their own souls or searching their own hearts. . . . I saw that all the religion a few poor souls have consists in watching the garments and acts of others, and finding fault with them. Unless they reform, there will be no place in heaven for them, for they would find fault with the Lord Himself."[14]

REFORMERS SO-CALLED

No matter what one says or does, there are some who are ready to criticize. "He can't start her!" declared a man as Robert Fulton attempted the first public demonstration of his steamboat. Finally steam and smoke belched forth, and the steamboat began to move. Startled, and no doubt disappointed, the critic was only a moment in taking up a new chant: "He can't stop her!"

"Satan has his work to accomplish, and he brings his power to bear most strongly at the great heart of the work. He seizes men and women who are selfish and unconsecrated, and makes of them sentinels to watch the faithful servants of God, to question their words, their actions, and their motives, and to find fault and murmur at their reproofs and warnings. Through them he creates suspicion and jealousy, and seeks to weaken the courage of the faithful, to please the unsanctified, and to bring to naught the labors of God's servants."[15]

Many people of the type described above call themselves reformers, but "reformers are not destroyers. They will never seek to ruin those who do not harmonize with their plans and assimilate to them. . . . A rude, condemnatory spirit is not essential to heroism in the reforms for this time."[16] "Those who feel at liberty to question and find fault with what God's servants are doing . . . may appear to be humble men; but they are self-deceived, and they deceive others. In their hearts are envy and evil surmising. They unsettle the faith of the people in those in whom they should have confidence, those whom God has chosen to do His work; and when they are reproved for their course they take it as personal abuse. While professing to be doing God's work they are in reality aiding the enemy."[17]

CRITICS NEED CONVERSION

Surely there is a time for constructive criticism, and even censure and reproof, to the right people, at the right time and place, and in the right way. But even these necessary duties of correction and discipline will bring pain, and not pleasure, to the converted man. He who finds "special enjoyment" in dealing with sin in any form gives evidence of an unconverted heart. "A heart where the peace of Christ is not, is unhappy, full of discontent; the person sees defects in everything, and he would bring discord into the most heavenly music. A life of selfishness is a life of evil. Those whose hearts are filled with love of self will store away evil thoughts of their brethren and will talk against God's instrumentalities. Passions kept warm and fierce by Satan's prompting are a bitter fountain, ever sending forth bitter streams to poison the life of others."[18]

The apostle Paul reminds us that "the unfruitful works of darkness" must be properly reproved, but beyond this "it is a shame even to speak of those things."

 IF SIN IS PLAIN IN A SISTER OR BROTHER, BREATHE IT NOT TO ANOTHER.

NOT SO FUNNY

"Don't ever make a fool of yourself and don't let others make a fool of you," counseled one of my theology professors at La Sierra University.

There is no one who can get more laughs than the minister, or church elder, if he "plays the fool" a bit. But have you noticed that when people want to get deep spiritual counsel, they don't often seek help from those who always have a funny story, who are "good Joes," or "jolly good fellows"? Have not you yourself lost a certain amount of confidence in church leaders who always have a nonsensical story to create a laugh? Have not some otherwise good sermons been spoiled because of too much humor?

RESERVED DIGNITY

It was Sabbath afternoon. There were more people than chairs in the living room. The elder, though urged to take a chair, humbly took a place on the carpet with the young people. His non-Seventh-day Adventist host was not noticeably chagrined, but I'll never forget the disappointed look on his face as this good elder proceeded to spend the hour amusing us with stories of the foolish pranks of his youth. "He [Christ] was highly social; yet He possessed a reserved dignity."[1]

Leaders in the church often forget how much people expect of them. I didn't see anything particularly wrong with the remarks of the master of ceremonies at the Christmas program, but my young secretary—a very "human" person herself—was horrified that an elder could tell so many jokes in one hour!

A STINKING SAVOR

On a similar occasion, how my respect rose for a minister who had the courage to forgo the laughs and give a serious speech after three other speakers had "brought the house down" with jokes and silly stories. Innocent humor is not out of order, but some of our humor is less innocent then we care to admit. "A little folly," says the wise man, "sends forth a stinking savor" from him who is otherwise "in reputation for wisdom and honor."[2]

Be happy, sunny, friendly and cheerful, but beware of excess and inappropriate humor.

 Key | **DON'T PAY TOO HIGH A PRICE FOR A LAUGH.**

PRACTICE WHAT YOU PREACH

"Do as I say, not as I do!" However desirous you may be that your child follow this counsel, she will seldom do any better than you do. One honest father told me he believed it was the inconsistencies in his own life that caused some of his children to drift from the church. Example is all-important in the home. And are we not often reminded by precept and, more painfully, by the lives of our members, that the church will seldom adopt a higher standard than that of her leaders?

WHITEWASH WON'T DO

To the world, also, it is apparent that "a man's character, like a fence, cannot be strengthened by whitewash." "It would be better for a worldling never to have seen a professor of religion than to come under the influence of one who is ignorant of the power of godliness."[1] "If you want your neighbor to know what Christ will do for him, let the neighbor see what Christ has done for you."[2]

"Sarvepalli Radhakrishnan, former president of India, [spoke] to a Christian missionary:

"'You Christians seem to us to be rather ordinary people making extraordinary claims.'

"Replied the missionary, 'We make these claims not for ourselves but for Jesus Christ.'

"Answered Radhakrishnan, 'If your Christ has not succeeded in making you into better men and women, have we any reason to suppose that He would do more for us?'"[3]

Most people know that "it is more important to watch how a man lives than to listen to what he says."[4] When I was a young boy, I stood one night by the entrance of a worldly place of amusement, a mental conflict raging between my desires to follow the crowd and the ideals set before me at church school. Who should walk past me and enter but the principal of the very school which I was attending! Though God still gave me the victory, how much harder it was because of a poor example! Have you and I been guilty also of practicing less than we preach?

PAY WITH THE SINNERS

"H. M. S. Richards, in his book *Feed My Sheep,* tells the story of a North Carolina preacher who lived some years ago when hotels entertained traveling ministers free of charge. This minister checked in at a small hotel in a little backwoods town, and for several days enjoyed the hospitality of the management. But when he started to leave, his host presented him with a bill. Surprised, he protested, 'Why, I thought preachers were entertained free.'

"'Well, yes they are,' the innkeeper replied, 'but you came and ate your meals without asking a blessing. No one has seen you with a Bible. You smoked the biggest cigars in the place. You talked about everything but religion. How do we know you are a preacher! You live like a sinner, and now you will have to pay with the sinners.'"[5]

Our literature evangelists are often reminded, "The people who purchase a book will read it, having before them a mental photograph of the face, conduct, and spirit of the man who sold it to them; and this silent influence will weigh heavily in the decisions they make for or against the truth."[6]

A FOOLISH BUILDER

"It is true, you may feel a sort of anxiety for the souls of those you love. You may seek to open to them the treasures of truth, and in your earnestness shed tears for their salvation; but when your words seem to make but little impression, and there is no apparent response to your prayers, you almost feel like casting reflection upon God that your labors bear no fruit. You feel that your dear ones have special hardness of heart, and that they do not respond to your efforts. But have you thought seriously that the fault may lie in your own self? Have you thought that you are pulling down with one hand that which you are striving to build up with the other?

"At times you have permitted the Spirit of God to have a controlling power over you, and at other times you have denied your faith by your practice . . . ; for your efforts in their behalf have been made of none effect by your practice. Your temper, your unspoken language, your manners, the repining state of your mind, your want of Christian fragrance, your want of spirituality, the very expression of your countenance, has witnessed against you." [7]

"Everyone occupies some kind of pulpit and preaches some sort of sermon every day."[8] After your praying and weeping and sermonizing are ended, what kind of message does your life preach? Can you picture a man laying bricks, putting up a brick with one hand and taking one down with the other? Quotation number seven above presents just such a picture and may help us discover why we are making little progress in helping others heavenward.

THE UNANSWERABLE ARGUMENT

"Our influence upon others depends not so much upon what we say as upon what we are. Men man combat and defy our logic, they may resist our appeals; but a life of disinterested love is an agrument they cannot gainsay,"[9]

Sincerity and a godly life will make up for many deficiencies in your work. Preaching and teaching may not be your calling. Your grammar may be poor, and even your understanding of the prophecies a bit confused. But you will still be preaching the most powerful sermon "in favor of the gospel" if you are a "loving and lovable Christian."[10]

That no man lives unto himself and that I am never justified in thinking my manner of life is "my own business," is well expressed in the following peom.

INTO MY GARDEN

Your seeds blow into my garden, friend,
    Whenever the wind is right;
They blow on wings of the wind by day,
    and they ride on the gales by night.
Whatever you grow in your garden, friend,
    Of beauty or ugly weed,
The fall will come, and the wind will blow,
    And over will come your seed.
Your words blow into my life, my friend;
    Or whether of good or ill,
Your thoughts fly over like ships of love,
    Or daggers that pierce and kill.
Your smiles blow into my heart, dear friend,
    And neighbors across the way,
Then blow and blossom in buds of love,
    A blessing to life all day.
Your life is a garden of love, dear friend,
    And planted with kindly deeds;
So ever over the fence will blow
    Into my garden your seeds.[11]

Remember, it was *"the life"* of Jesus which "was the light of men."[12] May His life be lived again in you and me that we too may be lights in this dark world.

Key | **PRACTICE WHAT YOU PREACH.**

THE PESSIMIST

"Life is an incurable disease," said Abraham Cowley. "Man's greatest crime is to have been born," contended De la Barce. How pessimistic, how morbid, how downright nauseatingly gloomy are the expressions of these seventeenth-century writers! Are we of the twentieth century guilty, perhaps unconsciously, of also looking on the dark side too often?

The Johannesburg Daily *Star* carried the story of Yugoslav truck driver Vojin Popovic, who sacrificed his life by looking on the darkest possible side of a bad situation.

His vehicle collided with a motorcycle carrying two people. Seeing the two lying under his truck, Popovic pulled out a revolver and shot himself.

The pair are still alive—the motorcyclist escaped with a slight head injury and the passenger, his wife, had only a broken leg. But the pessimist is dead! Surely we have everything to gain and nothing to lose by being optimistic and cheerful even during trying times.

LOOK ON THE BRIGHT SIDE

To those who in God's work are tempted to discouragement, Ellen White says, "Difficulties will arise that will try your faith and patience. Face them bravely. *Look on the bright side.* If the work is hindered, be sure that it is not your fault, and then go forward, rejoicing in the Lord."[1] If we can't say something hopeful or courageous, cheerful or optimistic, it would be better to say nothing.

> Talk faith. The world is better off without
> Your uttered ignorance and morbid doubt.
> If you have faith in God, or man, or self,
> Say so; if not, push back upon the shelf

Of silence all your thoughts till faith shall come;

No one will grieve because your lips are dumb.[2]

Some would argue that we must be a bit more realistic than the ninety-eight-year-old gentleman who had just had his annual birthday photograph taken. The young photographer said, "I hope I'll be around to take your picture when you're one hundred."

To this the old gentleman replied, "Why not? You look healthy to me."[3]

A mountain guide, the story goes, said to his party: "Don't go too near the edge of that precipice; it's dangerous. But if you do fall, remember to look to the left. You'll get a wonderful view!"[4] Is this carrying "looking on the bright side" a bit too far! Possibly. But it is still better than gloomy pessimism.

Have you met the person who seems to complain about everything? Things are either too sweet or too bitter, too long or too short, too fat or too thin, too much or too little, too hot or too cold, too wet or too dry. Someone described this type by saying, "A pessimist is a person who complains about the noise when opportunity knocks!"

"By continually dwelling on the dark side of their experiences, they [the Israelites] separated themselves farther and farther from God. They lost sight of the fact that but for their murmuring when the water ceased at Kadesh, they would have been spared the journey around Edom. God had purposed better things for them. Their hearts should have been filled with gratitude to Him that He had punished their sin so lightly. But instead of this, they flattered themselves that if God and Moses had not interfered, they might now have been in possession of the Promised Land. After bringing trouble upon themselves, making their lot altogether harder than God designed, they charged all their misfortunes upon Him. Thus they cherished bitter thoughts concerning His dealings with them, and finally they became discontented with everything."[5]

A LOVELY DAY

The day was wet and stormy. After morning prayer, a child was asked by his mother, "Why did you pray, 'Thank You for the lovely day'?" The child, so the story goes, replied, "Mother, you must learn never to judge a day by its weather!"

Though it may at times be difficult to look on the bright side when we are in the midst of trouble, surely we should not be weighed down with grief over things which have not yet happened. There is some consolation in the fact that if your dreams haven't come true, neither have your nightmares.

> Some of your hurts you have cured,
>
> And the sharpest you still have survived;
>
> But what torments of grief you endured
>
> From evils which never arrived!

"Sufficient unto the day is the evil thereof,"[6] said Jesus. Why add tomorrow's imaginary troubles to the real ones of today?

A WALK, A TALK, AND A JUMP

A man stood on the edge of a bridge, the story is told, ready to jump and end it all. A passerby persuaded him to go first for a walk with him and talk things over. Surely, things couldn't be so bad. If after the walk and talk he still wanted to jump, the promise was that he would not be prevented. After an hour of walking and talking, the story concludes, the two men came back to the bridge and both jumped! We who profess to have hope above all people, must not be carried along with the tide of others' discouragement's, but must exert a powerful, positive, hopeful influence.

MAKE A LEMONADE

Things may not always be entirely bright, but there is usually a brighter side at least. Play the Pollyanna game! If life hands you a lemon, make a lemonade. If your glass is half empty, don't complain; rather praise God that it is still half full. R. H. Pierson quoted Thomas Edison as saying, after 187 experiments failed, "Now we're making progress; we know 187 things that won't work!"

THE TOP OF THE HILL

I'd always live at the top of the hill,
Looking out at a beautiful scene.
I'd always live where the air is fresh
And the roads are pleasant and green.

But if I can't live at the top of the hill,
I'll live looking up and not down;
And if I must dwell in a crowded part
And walk through a dusty town,

I'll look for the sun in the ways of men,
And for space in a mind that is broad.
I'll watch for fragrance in human lives
And in hearts, for peace and concord.

Looking up and not down, looking forward,
    not back—
And there will be magic still
In the seeking and finding of beauty in life—
Just as if I lived up on the hill.[7]

"God does not want any to walk mournfully before Him."[8]

Key | **LOOK ON THE BRIGHT SIDE.**

BUSINESS IS MORE THAN BUSINESS

Speaking of some professed Christians, God, through the inspired pen, said, "They are full of zeal in worldly things, but they do not bring their religion into their business. They say: 'Religion is religion, and business is business.' They believe that each has its proper sphere, but they say: 'Let them be separated.'"[1] It is difficult to believe any Christian *really* thinks some part of his life can be lived apart from of his religion. But some must at least try to persuade themselves of this, or the above counsel would not have been written.

ONE HUNDRED PERCENT DISHONEST

"A store owner in Corpus Christi, Texas, discovered . . . that lie-detector tests often provide rather startling information. To help him evaluate potential employees, supermarket owner J. Franklin Critz gave lie-detector tests to all job applicants. The tests were entirely satisfactory in revealing attitudes toward money, work, drinking, and gambling. They also were helpful in providing a picture of applicants' ability to get along with other members of the staff. But on the question of honesty Mr. Critz reported: 'In the first test in the first store 100 percent of the employees were found to be dishonest. So we decided to overlook all but the extreme cases.'"[2]

We expect to find dishonesty in the world. We preach that outside the Holy City will be found "whosoever loveth and maketh a lie,"[3] but maybe some of us who are "in the church" are still more "of the world" than we realize. Is the following counsel now out of date? "Dishonesty is practiced all through our ranks, and this is the cause of lukewarmness on the part of many who profess to believe the truth. They are not connected with Christ and are deceiving their own souls. I am pained to make the statement that there is an alarming lack of honesty even among Sabbath keepers."[4]

MELTING MONEY

In the following little story are found principles worth pondering: "Emperor Frederick the Great often experienced considerable difficulty in balancing his country's budget. On one occasion he gave a dinner, inviting prominent men of the empire to discuss the situation. He explained his dilemma and inquired how it could come about that, although taxes were quite high, not enough money reached the desired objectives.

"At length an old general arose in the midst of the discussion, silently fished a large lump of ice from the punch bowl, handed it to this neighbor, and suggested that it be passed around the table until it reached the emperor. This was done, and by the time the ice got to Frederick it was no larger than a small walnut.

"The lesson was obvious: the national revenues were passing through too many hands, and everybody kept some until graft had consumed the major portion.

"It is both strange and unfortunate that somebody else's money seems to stick to our fingers like iron filings to a magnet. Particularly if it is government money, we seem to assume that we have as much right to it as anyone else, since we paid our share of the taxes going into the funds.

"If I possess the proper amount of integrity, I shall be as honest in the use of other people's money as in that of my own. 'I shall not take it, for it is not mine. It is a trust in my hands, and I shall, at all costs, be a good steward."[5]

We will never get on well with fellow members, fellow workers, or the people of the world, nor will we witness effectively to them, while we are in any way dishonest.

LITTLE THINGS

C. L. Paddock tells of a young man who was in line for promotion to a more responsible position in the bank where he was employed. At the cafeteria one day this young man slipped a pat of butter under his bread to avoid paying for it. One of the bank directors saw him. He failed to receive the promotion.[6]

A little thing? Possibly. But Jesus revealed the magnitude of that which we may call little when He said, "He that is faithful in that which is least is faithful also in much: and he that is unjust in the least is unjust also in much."[7] Said Sir Walter Scott, "O what a tangled web we weave when first we practice to deceive!" We are in danger when we make the slightest approach to dishonesty.

GAINING BY LOSING

Though the inspired writings often urge us to be frugal, not spending money foolishly and carelessly, we are also told there are some things more important than saving money. "Some of the Sabbath keepers who say to the world that they are looking for Jesus' coming, and that they believe we are having the last message of mercy, give way to their natural feelings, and barter, and trade, and are a proverb among unbelievers for their keenness in trade, for being sharp, and always getting the best end of the bargain. Such would better lose a little and exert a better influence in the world, and a happier influence among brethren, and show that this world is not their god."[8]

Does it surprise you that the Lord actually counsels us to "lose a little" money for the sake of a better influence?

LEST WE OFFEND

Jesus taught us that we should be more concerned with good human relations than with money. He was not in any way obliged to pay the tax in question, but he told Peter, "Notwithstanding, *lest we should offend them,*"[9] pay the tax.

Let our business conduct be dictated less by gold than by the golden rule. Do we forget in our joy over a "good deal" that when we get something for nothing, someone else gets nothing for something?

It is the purpose of God to glorify Himself in His people before the world. . . . The religion of Christ is to be interwoven with all that they do and say. Their every business transaction is to be fragrant with the presence of God."[10]

Let us remember that we are in this world not to gain money, but to gain the kingdom and to help others enter in as well. Nor are we here so much to watch the pennies, as to watch for souls. Our own souls, or the souls of others, are worth far more than any wealth we might gain by dishonesty—worth more than anything we might lose by giving the other person the better end of the bargain.

> **Key** | *REMEMBER BUSINESS AND RELIGION CANNOT BE SEPARATED.*

POSITION SEEKERS

An onion once decided that he was not an onion at all, but a tulip bulb. And so he boasted loudly to the other onions that he was better than they—that he would grow into a gorgeous tulip. Eventually he was planted; he grew, and proved after all to be a little onion! After this he became the laughingstock of the garden, and he died at an early age. He lost his chance to be a superior sort of onion—forgetting in his fruitless ambition that there is need in the world for both onions and tulips.[1]

"Do not pass by the little things and look for a large work. You might do successfully the small work, but fail utterly in attempting a larger work and fall into discouragement. Take hold wherever you see that there is work to be done. It will be by doing with your might what your hands find to do that you will develop talents and aptitude for a larger work. It is by slighting the daily opportunities, neglecting the little things, that so many become fruitless and withered."[2]

How many problems could be avoided in the work of the church were every man content with his position, remembering that "promotion cometh neither from the east, nor from the west, nor from the south. But God is the judge: He putteth down one, and setteth up another."[3] All accusations that the brethren have made a mistake in passing us by will be silenced when we know that "if any are qualified for a higher position, the Lord will lay the burden, not alone on them, but on those who have tested them, who know their worth, and who can understandingly urge them forward."[4]

If God has called us to our work, and if this is truly His work, can we not trust Him to see that we are "called" to the right place at the right time? I always feel a bit sorry for ministerial students who seem to worry quite a lot about the time when the "calls" will be passed out. Is it too childish or naive to believe if God has called us to prepare for the ministry, he will provide a place for us to minister? "Not more surely is the place prepared for us in the heavenly mansions than is the special place designated on earth where we are to work for God."[5]

This applies to *every* Christian, does it not?

RESTLESS FEET

God's "special place" for me was in the literature ministry in the state of Utah where, after three months of successful work, I would become assistant publishing secretary. This "designated" place was shown to me by a "call" from the brethren and by a deep conviction. I have never doubted that God led me in just the way I would desire to be led could I see the end from the beginning.

And since that time I have found my sometimes restless feet wise in following the counsel: "Suffer nothing to divide your interest from your present work until God shall see fit to give you another piece of work. . . ."[6]

CROWN OR CROSS

"Seekest thou great things for thyself? seek them not."[7] "The Lord has no place in His work for those who have a greater desire to win the crown than to bear the cross. He wants men who are more intent upon doing their duty than upon receiving their reward—men who are more solicitous for principle than for promotion."[8]

Oh that our concern for the souls placed within our care would so consume us that position could not enter our minds! Our Redeemer, who could by right have abandoned us to die alone while He returned to His exalted place at the right hand of God, was "so devoted . . . to the work of saving souls that *He even longed* for His baptism of blood."[9] What selfless love! Does it not cause us all to hang our heads in shame?

We have all known the man who volunteers for a position, who asks his friends to put in a good word for him, and then when passed by, wails, "If the brethern only knew my qualifications!" There may be times when we are pushed aside or neglected without good cause, but it is always more safe to examine ourselves to see if the fault lies with us. "We need to beware of self-pity. Never indulge the feeling that you are not esteemed as you should be, that your efforts are not appreciated."[10]

THE WRONG METHOD

"KICK YOUR WAY TO FAME!" These words in a shop window full of soccer shoes on Main Street, Cape Town, caught my attention one evening while I was waiting for a train. While this may be a legitimate way to become famous in football or soccer, surely we can only mourn the fact that this method has also been used in an attempt for fame in God's work. Listen carefully: "The envious man diffuses poison wherever he goes, alienating friends and stirring up hatred and rebellion against God and man. He seeks to be thought best and greatest, not by putting forth heroic, self-denying efforts to reach the goal of excellence himself, but by standing where he is and diminishing the merit due to the efforts of others." "The envious man shuts his eyes to the good qualities and noble deeds of others. He is always ready to disparage and misrepresent that which is excellent."[11]

HONORED OR HONORABLE

Wrote Shakespeare, "I am not covetous for gold; but if it be a sin to covet honor, I am the most offending soul alive." While we may not know just what Shakespeare had in mind when he penned these words, it would seem that perhaps he wanted to be *honorable,* rather than just to be *honored*—to deserve honor rather than demand it. In this there is no wrong. "Have you thoughts that you dare not express, that you may one day stand upon the summit of intellectual greatness; that you may sit in deliberative and legislative councils, and help to enact laws for the nation? There is nothing wrong in these aspirations. You may every one of you make your mark. You should be content with no mean attainments. Aim high, and spare no pains to reach the standard."[12]

No, it is not wrong to qualify oneself for high position, but we are to prepare faithfully and continuously and leave with God and with those who know our worth, and who can understandingly urge us forward, the decision as to when we are ready for these higher positions.

DESERVE SUCCESS

"The best way to get out of a lowly position is to be consistently effective in it,"[13] said someone wise. And over 200 years ago, Joseph Addison wrote, "Tis not in mortals to command success, but we'll do more,—we'll deserve it." "Satan selects his disciples when they are idle; but Christ chose His when they were busy at their work, either mending their nets, or casting them into the sea."[14] "It is those who perform faithfully their appointed work day by day, who in God's own time will hear His call, 'Come up higher,'"[15] If we do not keep busy in our present appointed task, we may forever miss the secret of success in life which, Disraeli said, "is for a man to be ready for his opportunity when it comes."[16]

A genuine reluctance and feeling of unreadiness for position can often be one important sign that you are qualified. Speaking of young men who walk and talk with God and work diligently where they are, the servant of the Lord says, "When there are vacancies to be filled, you will hear the words, Friend, come up higher. *You may be reluctant to advance, but move forward* with trust in God, bringing into His work a fresh, honest experience and a heart filled with the faith that works by love and purifies the soul."[17]

VOLUNTEERS AND DRAFTEES

A young man hesitated about accepting an invitation to be publishing secretary of a rather large conference. A still younger man with far less experience advised, "I know what I'd do; I'd jump at the chance." Strange though it may seem, the eager, courageous-appearing volunteers do not always make the best soldiers. Many a hero has been made of a self-distrustful draftee who might never have joined had the decision been left up to him. Yet once drafted or called, appointed or assigned, a courageous hero may be born from him who may even think of himself as somewhat of a coward! To be able to say, "Here I am—not by choice but by appointment, not by 'pulling strings' but by unsolicited invitation, not because of a thirst for fame but from sense of duty"—brings strength out of apparent weakness. " Humble yourselves therefore under the mighty hand of God, that He may exalt you in due time."[18]

"Brethren, if you continue to be as idle, as worldly, as selfish as you have been, God will surely pass you by, and take those who are less self-caring, less ambitious for worldly honor, and who will not hesitate to go, as did their Master, without the camp, bearing the reproach. The work will be given to those who will take it, those who prize it, who weave its principles into their everyday experience. God will choose humble men who are seeking to glorify His name and advance His cause rather than to honor and advance themselves. He will raise up men who have not so much worldly wisdom, but who are connected with Him, and who will seek strength and counsel from above."[19]

WHO IS THE GREATEST?

A much-traveled and well-known priest humbly wondered if the man who travels 20,000 miles for God is not less of a hero than the man who stays 20,000 days in the same place. He may be closer to God's viewpoint than most of us. The following quotation, while rebuking the ambitious, restless minister, should bring courage and comfort to the faithful church or lay worker who feels unnoticed and unimportant. "Among many of the ministers of Christ there is a feeling of unrest, . . . a desire to do something great, to create a sensation, to be accounted able speakers, and to gain for themselves honor and distinction. If such could encounter perils and receive the honor given to heroes, they would engage in the work with unflagging energy. But to live and labor almost unknown, to toil and sacrifice for Jesus in obscurity, receiving no special praise from men—this requires a soundness of principle and a steadfastness of purpose that but few possess. Were there a greater effort to walk humbly with God, looking away from men and laboring only for Christ's sake, far more would be accomplished."[20]

THE VINEYARD

There are many who go to the vineyard
    To answer the call of the Lord,
With an eye not alone to the labor,
    But looking for great reward.

They will work with zest near the highways
    Where those passing by may see,
But will drop from the ranks in a moment
    If placed in obscurity.

Yet the vines at the back of the vineyard
    Were planted with equal care,
And the Master has never forgotten
    How many He planted there.

And the Lord who has called us to labor
    Knows best what each one can do,
So be quick to go out in the vineyard
    Though no one may notice you.

For the grapes at the back of the garden
    May grow on a precious stalk
That the Lord would not plant near the roadside
    Where thieves and the thoughtless walk.

And the place where He bids you to labor
    May seem a forsaken plot,
But prove out in the plan of the Master
    A specially cherished spot.
Then go out to the place He has given,
    Nor question His high decree;
But be true to your task till the end of time,
    Though no one may know or see.

The grapes on your side of the vineyard
    May prove to be Eschol's brand,
When the labor is done and the workers
    Before Him shall take their stand.[21]

Key | ***WORK HARD WHERE YOU ARE—KEEP IMPROVING, BUT LEAVE PROMOTIONS TO GOD.***

FORGIVE

She related the injustices done her by another sister. Detecting bitterness in her voice, I said, "I hope you have forgiven her." She exploded, "I'll never forgive until she says she's sorry! The Bible says we must confess our sins before we can be forgiven!"

While it is true we must confess our sins before we can receive forgiveness from God, we must ever know forgiveness is already in God's heart only awaiting our reception. God is holding no grudge against us until we confess. Godlikeness must be our standard in dealing with our fellowman.

I ALREADY HAVE

As well as illustrating how a parent ought *not* to deal with his children, the following story can teach us something about forgiveness. I punished by mistake my five-year-old son when his younger brother was the one guilty of serious mischief. I was not long in learning I had done wrong. How could I persuade the unjustly punished son to forgive me? The tears still flowed. The punishment had been rather severe, and he keenly sensed the injustice done him. I took him on my lap, confessed my mistake, and reminded him of his current Sabbath School memory verse, "Forgive, and ye shall be forgiven." I hoped thereby to prepare him to forgive my foolish error. All of this was unnecessary. When I finally said, "Please forgive me," he replied through tears, and I shall never forget the words, "I already have."

"I already have!" What beautiful words. "Except ye be converted, and become as little children, ye shall not enter into the kingdom of heaven."[1]

Surely, when we come to Jesus with broken and contrite hearts pleading forgiveness for the worst of sins, He answers, "I already have forgiven you." Even as the soldiers knelt beside Jesus, not in humility and penitence, but cruelly driving nails through His hands and feet, He prayed, "Father, forgive them; for they know not what they do."[2] Perhaps some of them later accepted Him as their Saviour. When they confessed and asked Him to forgive them, I am certain the answer was ready, "I already have."

TRUE FORGIVENESS

"Beloved, if God so loved us, we ought also to love one another."[3] We cannot make others love us or confess to us, but if we have hatred in our hearts toward someone even for real wrongs which he has committed against us, we are in danger of the judgment. "Nothing can justify an unforgiving spirit. He who is unmerciful toward others shows that he himself is not a partaker of God's pardoning grace."[4] The person who withholds love and forgiveness until her enemy comes in confession will be wholly incapable of forgiving her even if she should come crawling in the dust!

Let's face the facts: Most of those who have wronged us will never confess. Now suppose I should come to death's door. I love only those who have either done me no wrong or who have confessed to me. All others I regard with bitterness and hatred. What then? Can I die like that and find entrance into heaven to meet the One face to face who, "while we were yet sinners," "died for us"?[5]

What were the feelings of the One who had never committed an offense against anyone as He knelt washing the feet of the man who would betray Him for thirty pieces of silver? Was it not the love and forgiveness in the very touch of Jesus' hands that sent a thrill through the soul of Judas and brought him near repentance?[6] Even if the results of the betrayal had remained very much the same, I am certain Jesus would have accepted a penitent Judas at any time. With open arms He would have assured, "I already have forgiven you!"

LOVE NOT A REACTION

As we from time to time kneel to wash one another's feet, it is not enough to wash *someone's* feet. We must, in heart, wash everyone's feet. You cannot really love anyone until you love everyone, for when that one whom you think you love displeases or turns against you, you will hate him too.

Love is not dependent upon the actions of others. Real love is a positive outreach which will embrace even the unlovely and those who hate us. God's love, which must be manifest in us, is not a reaction to the goodness, kindness, and lovableness of others. This type of affection, which is as changeable as is its object, may be very real and somewhat satisfying, but is not enduring enough for eternity.

If I cannot wash everyone's feet—friend or enemy, rich or poor, black or white, clean or unclean—then have I really partaken of the flesh and blood of Christ for the covering of my sins! "Forgive, and ye shall be forgiven."[7]

And I wonder if some of us will not be held, to some degree, responsible for the failure of some to confess their wrongs. Souls may be eternally lost simply because it was quite evident that forgiveness was not available to them even should they confess to us.

How much happier life would be if we could only be more forgiving.

Key	*FORGIVE ONE ANOTHER.*

DO YOU EXPECT TOO MUCH OF OTHERS?

It certainly is not wrong for us to expect great things of ourselves (even this, if overdone, can lead to disillusionment); but we will avoid disappointment and frustration if we do not expect too much of others. The fact is, we often expect far more of others than we would want them to expect of us if our situations were reversed. We are usually not conscious of the fact that we are making unreasonable demands on people. We do not intend to harm anyone—but we do.

Dr. Wilfred J. Airey took time enough during a history class to say, and I don't think he'll mind if I quote him, "One of the problems at a school like this is that we expect mature behavior of people who are not yet mature." Thinking myself quite mature, as most college students do, I wasn't altogether sure I knew what he meant. But with the passing of years since graduation day, I've begun to understand.

The admonition, "Remember, you were young once too," becomes more necessary with every passing year. When I do remember to remember, I realize the silly things boys do and say and laugh at today are little more or less than an echo of their father's youthful behavior. The ideas and questions of modern youth reflect thoughts similar to those Dad had twenty or thirty years ago. The current desire of some to receive an education by doing little more than paying the fees is not so current after all. The common failure of even the best of youth to express gratitude to parent, teacher, and preacher for endless sacrifice and effort in their behalf is nothing new. The same problems continue.

Have we forgotten how we ourselves prayed for the colporteurs long before we knew what they were? And how confusing "simple" Bible expressions were? I recall, as a young person making the astounding discovery that the then current undersea earthquakes were predicted in the Bible. "Earthquakes in divers places"—where else do "divers" go but to the bottom of the sea!

I'm glad the pastor of the Sacramento Central Church during my teen years did not cease his efforts to "break through" to the boys whose parents allowed them to sit in the back rows of the balcony. It was there that I made my decision and unobtrusively slipped my name into the offering plate requesting baptism.

When Elder A. V. Bentz responded with a visit to my home, I'm glad he did not appear shocked when he found I was not sure whether the second advent (or was it the resurrection of the righteous?) occurred before or after the millennium. I didn't even understand the question, much less know the answer! I had not been reared in Sabbath School and attended church school for the first time only the following year. But I've always been sure Elder Bentz did right by baptizing me when my desire to "make a committment" was fresh and strong, regardless of my ignorance.

DOGS OR DADDIES

Parents often expect more than mature thought in their children. In telling my boys about a South American ship disaster of July, 1963, in which our Pastor Rasi lost his life and in which Pastor R. Curtis Barger almost lost his, I referred to the newspaper account: "Several survivors said several men pushed women from lifeboats to save personal belongings." I asked my kindergarten-age son, "What would you have done if you were on that lifeboat with your brand-new bicycle and there wasn't room for all the people *and* your bicycle?" He first suggested that he would hold the bicycle on his lap. Then, noting my disappointment at his hesitance to give a straightforward reply, he quickly turned on me: "And, daddy, what would you do if you were there in the water with a cute little tiny dog? And there wasn't room for both of you in the boat?"

I got the point and changed the subject. Some questions are hard to answer. How can I expect a young child to know that a jettisoned bicycle can be more easily replaced than a drowned stranger? And how do you explain to a little boy that daddies are worth more than his cuddly "cute little tiny dog"?

YOUNG EXPECT TOO MUCH OF OLD

Yes, the old expect too much of the young, but the young frequently expect too much of the old. It has taken all too long for some of us to conquer our childish habit of expecting godlike behavior of our elders. Far too late in life do many of us stop criticizing and start helping, stop judging sinners and start leading them to Him who says, "Neither do I condemn thee." [1]

How slowly it dawns on some that we are *all* a part of the problem of sin. Students *and* teachers, congregation *and* preacher, child *and* parent are alike locked in deadly struggle with the enemy of all good. We all need help, regardless of profession, position, or seniority.

A mother may be lost because of children who expect too much of her, condemning and rejecting her when they should have risen to help her by understanding, encouragement, and prayer. And are there fathers who will finally go to their graves with heavy hearts because of children who were disappointed in them, who could not find it in their hearts to forgive, who discovered too late that fathers are human beings and not gods?

Many a minister has fallen by the wayside because church members expected him to be superhuman, beyond the need of sympathy and encouragement, understanding and pardon. Have not teachers become discouraged because of students who didn't appreciate their sacrifice and efforts, their dedication and patience?

IN A STRANGE CHURCH

And don't we take far too much for granted when working for those not of our faith? Do we wonder why they don't attend our church so readily even though they seem interested and we invite them repeatedly? Some even promise to come but never turn up. Are they insincere and just afraid to tell us they're not interested?

In Cape Town I visited a church of a certain faith for the first time. I was quite sure strangers were welcome and I would be expected to "make myself at home," but I had a strange sense of stage fright, or the like, as I approached the door. I wondered if I would know when to kneel, stand, and sit. Suppose I got into someone else's pew.

When I sat down, I failed to bow my head, but noticed those who came in after me bowed far forward leaning their head on the back of the pew in front of them, for quite a time. What would they think of my irreverence if they learned I was a Seventh-day Adventist! If I passed up the bread and wine would I be considered a heathen? If I partook, would I be seen as an over-assuming stranger?

People seemed to note that I was new there, and I felt uncomfortable when they stared at me. I even wondered for a moment if I was dressed appropriately, whether my tie was too "loud." The service being rather formal and unannounced, I found myself once in the attitude of prayer when the minister was only reading.

The fact that I felt a bit relieved when the service ended before I had opportunity to make more blunders, set me to thinking about those who visit our church for the first time. We can well be surprised when new people turn up on their own and make themselves at home in our church! It takes courage, especially for those who know that anything from a wedding ring to the smell of smoke may offend some sensitive soul.

WHO'S WITHOUT EXCUSE

Since this experience, I have read with new understanding the warning that "we become too easily discouraged over the souls who do not at once respond to our efforts."[2]

Let us remember, too, that many of those intelligent people whom we think know what we believe really do not. Not long after I completed college a man startled me with this: "The Bible says the seventh day of the week is the Sabbath, so why do you Seventh-day Adventists keep Saturday?" Taken aback for a moment, I recovered and referred him to the calendar above his head. A few seconds later he faced me with an expression of sheer shock. "I've never seen that before!" he declared.

How cautiously we should approach the conclusion, "They know what we believe. They'll have to decide for themselves." Never judge anyone as "without excuse." It may be we who will be found without excuse for expecting too much of others. "*Never* should we cease to labor for a soul while there is one gleam of hope. Precious souls cost our self-sacrificing Redeemer too dear a price to be lightly given up to the tempter's power."[3]

IN ANOTHER'S MOCCASINS

Don't be alarmed when people seem to fight against the truth which has just begun to dawn upon them. How true are the words of Doreen Fox in her article, Winsome Ways With Roman Catholics. "It is necessary to walk in the other's moccasins and think how we would feel if someone seemed to be able to prove that the 2300-day prophecy was baseless, that the Sabbath was nothing more than a Jewish myth. How shaken and bewildered we would be."[4]

How conscientious I was only weeks before my baptism to wait until sundown to attend my Saturday afternoon movie! I did quit the movie habit before I was baptized, but fortunately some over-zealous critic didn't see me standing across the street from the theater waiting for the sun to disappear. I may not have been well informed, but I was sincere in following the convictions which fastened themselves one by one upon my heart.

Even within the church we should be very tolerant of those who don't see things which are so obvious to us. We are like so many children, not all having been "born" at the same time nor "growing" at the same rate nor thriving on the same "food."

Even when our growth is complete on this earth, we will not all be the same in stature. Beyond minimum standards let us live and let live; love and let God be the judge of every person's growth and experience.

What irreparable harm has been done by those who make their own Christian maturity a standard by which to judge all others!

Key | *DON'T EXPECT TOO MUCH OF OTHERS.*

THE SECRET TO BETTER HUMAN RELATIONS NOW

The secret of rapid development in the field of human relations is to adopt the heavenly standard as your goal here and now. "If you are to be saints in heaven, you must first be saints upon the earth."[1] Be satisfied with nothing less. God, then, in His mercy, will test you in the world, more closely in the church, and still more closely in the home, until you, by His grace, reflect the perfect human nature of Jesus.

HEAVENLY HUMAN RELATIONS

Surely the ideal in human relations will be reached only in the new earth. Can you imagine anyone losing his temper in heaven—giving someone a piece of his mind? What would you think if Peter pulled you aside and shared a bit of gossip with you about John's youthful days? Is it likely that Barnabas would feel that he simply must tell you how wrong Paul was in their argument over John Mark? Can you picture yourself in the abodes of bliss complaining to the angel Gabriel that your inheritance is not as large as that of the person who worked under you on earth? Could tribal, national, and racial conflicts enter there? Surely, if "God's ideal for His children" is "higher than the highest human thought can reach,"[2] and if we are to be preparing here for heaven, then we have some improvement to make in our dealings with our fellow creatures.

A SEVERE TEST

The highest step on the ladder toward "heavenly human relationships" is in the home. Is not home to be a little heaven on earth? And is it not here that the test of our true character is the most severe? Here we develop the finer points of good character: genuine love and patience and kindness toward those who must accept us no matter how we act. A person is no better than he or she is at home.

One man said, "My home and family are ruining me!" Doubtless he should have said his home relationships were bringing out the worst of his character and helping him to see himself as God sees him. While it is true that the close contacts in the home will often be a real trial to a person's character, it cannot bring out of one that which is not *in* them. Indeed, God in His great mercy reveals to us these traits that we may overcome them and have happier lives and be more effective in our service to others. "The church needs men of a meek and quiet spirit, who are long-suffering and patient. Let them learn these attributes in dealing with their families."[3]

"The characters we form will speak in the home life. If there is sweet accord in the home circle, the angels of God may minister in the home. If there is wise management at home— kindness, meekness, forbearance, combined with firm principles—then be assured that the husband is a house band; he binds the family together with holy cords and presents them to God, binding himself with them upon the altar of god. What a light shines forth from such a family!

"That family, properly conducted, is a favorable argument to the truth, and the head of such a family will carry out the very same kind of work in the church as is revealed in the family. Wherever severity, harshness, and want of affection and love are exhibited in the sacred circle of the home, there will most assuredly be a failure in the plans and management in the church."[4]

So the home is, among other things, a proving ground and a training school to fit us for effective service in the gospel field and in heaven. A man is no better outside than he is inside his home. He may put on a better "front," but people cannot be wholly deceived. Whenever you hear yourself speaking in less than kind tones to wife or child, remember *that this is your true self.* (Most of us try to console ourselves, when we think of our un-Christlike words and acts, by saying, "I just wasn't myself!")

IN THE CHURCH

The next rung below, on the ladder to perfect human relationships, will be the test of our "charity for all" in the church. A man may appear to the church to be better in his human relationships than he appears to his wife and children; nevertheless, the test of his real character here is much more close and exacting than in the "world." In the church, somewhat as in the home, a man is with those from whom he generally seeks no special favors, with people who *must* love or at least tolerate him. How do we conduct ourselves in such a situation?

IN THE WORLD

The "world" we will accept as the lowest round of the ladder. Here a man who is a critic in the church, a tyrant on committees, a demon at home, and totally unfit for dwelling peacefully in heaven, can still often make his way by following certain rules for winning friends and influencing people. He can have relative success by outward politeness and pretended interest in others.

Being satisfied with getting along in the world but not in the church will never do. Getting along with the brethren but not with wife and children is not service which heaven can approve. And to be tolerant and tolerable at home is not enough to bring us into harmony with the atmosphere of heaven. We must be "not of this world," even now. We must be otherworldly—heavenly minded. Then family, church, and world will take knowledge of us that we have been with Jesus and know that we plan to spend eternity with Him.

HAVE WE STUDIED IN VAIN?

We have by no means exhausted the study of the reasons why we have problems in dealing with people—at home, in the church, and in the world. But even what we have studied will have been studied in vain if we have not been brought to our knees in rededication to the goal of allowing the Word of God to be lived out completely within our lives.

We, with Jesus, want to go "about doing good"[5] and not evil in all our contacts with men. "Every day's experience was an outpouring of His life. In one way only could such a life be sustained. Jesus lived in dependence upon God and communion with Him. To the secret place of the Most High, under the shadow of the Almighty, men now and then repair; they abide for a season, and the result is manifest in noble deeds; then their faith fails, the communion is interrupted, and the lifework marred."[6]

The lifework and communion with God cannot be separated. Never has a worthwhile contribution been made to God's work by one who is not living a life of prayer. "Only the work accomplished with much prayer, and sanctified by the merit of Christ, will in the end prove to have been efficient for good."[7] All prayerless efforts are not only of no value to, but actually hinder, the cause of God. "It is easier for many to talk than to pray; such lack spirituality and holiness, and their influence is an injury to the cause of God."[8]

TOO BUSY TO PRAY

Are we too busy to pray and study God's Word each day? We could save hours of time if we did. Luther once said, "I have so much to do today that I must spend at least four hours in prayer before I begin." "Before our brethren assemble in council or board meetings, each one should present himself before God, carefully searching the heart and critically examining the motives. Pray that the Lord may reveal self to you so that you may not unwisely criticize or condemn propositions."[9] How many committee meetings would be shortened, how many unwise words remain unspoken, how many decisions could remain unreversed, how many brethren would remain close to one another, if all workers in the church followed this counsel!

Do you feel that you can't take more time for communion with God because you are always behind with your work? Listen: "The reason why our preachers accomplish so little is that they do not walk with God. He is a day's journey from most of them."[10] "No man, high or low, experienced or inexperienced, can steadily maintain before his fellowmen a pure, forceful life unless his life is hid with Christ in God. The greater the activity among men, the closer should be the communion of the heart with God."[11]

"Many fail of imitating our holy Pattern because they study so little the definite features of that character. So many are full of busy plans, always active; and there is no time or place for the precious Jesus to be a close, dear companion. They do not refer every thought and action to Him, inquiring: 'Is this the way of the Lord!' If they did they would walk with God, as did Enoch."[12]

"Nothing is more needed in our work than the practical results of communion with God."[13] Here will be found the best answer to our every "people problem."

REFERENCES

Introduction: Why Study Human Relations?   page vii

1. John 13:35.

2. Luke 2:52. See also 1 Samuel 2:26.

3. *Messages for Young People*, p. 405.

4. *Christ's Object Lessons*, p. 339.

Love Everybody?   pages 9 - 12

1. *Christ's Object Lesson*, p. 384.

2. See Philippians 2:5.

3. Romans 5:20.

4. *Testimonies*, vol. 5, pp. 612, 613.

5. *The Desire of Ages*, p. 191.

6. *Christ's Object Lessons*, p. 384.

7. *The Desire of Ages*, p. 668.

8. Galatians 2:20.

Tell It Like It Is?   pages 13 - 16

1. *Evangelism*, pp. 539, 540.

2. *Ibid.*, p. 540.

3. *Ibid.*, p. 542, 543.

4. *Ibid.*, p. 543.

Do You Talk Too Much?   pages 17 - 18

1. *Sunshine Magazine*, February, 1964.

2. *Ibid.*, July, 1963.

3. Mark 1:44, 45.

4. *Evangelism*, pp. 653, 654.

You're Not Listening   pages 21 - 23

1. Ecclesiastes 5:1, 2.

2. *The Desire of Ages*, p. 524.

Thoughtless Words   pages 24 - 26

1. Proverbs 30:32.

2. Proverbs 29:11.

3. Psalm 19:14.

4. James 3:2.

5. Colporteur Ministry, p. 73.

6. Education, pp. 236, 237.

7. 1 Corinthians 10:11.

Change That Tone   pages 27 - 28

1. *Child Guidance*, p. 240.
2. *The Desire of Ages*, p. 353 (Emphasis added.)
3. *Testimonies*, vol. 4, p. 66.
4. *The Sanctified Life*, p. 16. (Emphasis added.)
5. Colossians 4:6.

Try Smiling   pages 29 - 33

1. Verna Fuller Young, *Sunshine Magazine*, September, 1963.
2. *Ibid.*, August, 1963.
3. *Steps to Christ*, pp. 120, 121. (Emphasis added.)
4. *Child Guidance*, pp. 147, 148.

Be Humble   pages 34 - 36

1. Proverbs 16:18. 19.
2. *Sunshine Magazine*, October, 1963.
3. *Counsels on Sabbath School Work*, p. 91.
4. *Sunshine Magazine*, December, 1963.
5. *Testimonies*, vol. 4, p. 608.
6. Proverbs 15:33.
7. *The Desire of Ages*, p. 436.
8. *Ibid.*
9. *Evangelism*, p. 596.
10. *Prophets and Kings*, p. 30.

When Others Don't See Things Your Way   pages 37 - 39

1. *Testimonies*, vol. 4, p. 65.
2. *Ibid.*, vol. 5, pp. 461, 462.
3. 1 Corinthians 9:22.

If I Could Just Get Organized   pages 40 - 43

1. Credited to Douglas Malloch by Daryl V. Hoole, *The Art of Homemaking*, Deseret Book Company, Salt Lake City.
2. *Testimonies to Ministers*, p. 28.
3. *Evangelism*, p. 94.
4. *Testimony Treasures*, vol. 2, p. 459.
5. *Testimonies*, vol. 3, p. 195.
6. *Evangelism*, p. 649.
7. *Messages to Young People*, p. 101.
8. *Evangelism*, p. 650.
9. *Gospel Workers*, p. 278.
10. *Evangelism*, p. 652.

Look Your Best   pages 44 - 45

1. *Messages to Young People,* pp. 349, 350. (Emphasis added.)
2. *Child Guidance,* p. 415.
3. *Evangelism,* p. 671. (Emphasis added.)
4. *The Ministry of Healing,* p. 289.
5. *Testimonies,* vol. 6, p. 96.
6. *Child Guidance,* p. 415.
7. *Ibid.,* 425.

To Be Young   pages 46 - 48

1. Kenneth Wood, Jr., *Meditations for Moderns,* p. 296.
2. Curtis Quackenbush, *"The Essential Preparation," Review and Herald,* August 6, 1964.
3. Dr. G. S. Ross, *Sunshine Magazine,* October, 1963. (Emphasis added.)
4. Proverbs 9:8, 9.
5. *Sunshine Magazine,* January, 1963.
6. *Ibid.,* August, 1963.

Courage To Be Wrong   pages 49 - 51

1. *Review and Herald,* December 16, 1884.
2. *Sunshine Magazine,* June, 1962.
3. *Testimonies,* vol. 3, pp. 527, 528.
4. *Early Writings,* p. 119.
5. *Sunshine Magazine,* July, 1963.
6. *Ibid.,* June, 1964.
7. *Ibid.,* August, 1964.
8. *The Ministry,* December, 1964.
9. *Sunshine Magazine,* August, 1965.
10. 1 Samuel 25:32, 33.
11. *Patriarchs and Prophets,* p. 667.

Playing Favorites   pages 52 - 55

1. C. L Paddock, *"A Serious Mistake," Review and Herald,* May 6, 1965.
2. *Ibid.*
3. *Christ's Object Lessons,* p. 376.
4. *The Ministry of Healing,* p. 489.
5. Romans 5:10.
6. Job 42:10; 32:1.

Sour Stomachs and Words   pages 56 - 57

1. E. G. White, *My Life Today,* p. 97.
2. *Testimonies,* vol. 7, pp. 257, 258.

Say Thank You   pages 58 - 60

1. *Patriarchs and Prophets,* p. 219. (Emphasis added.)
2. *Christ's Object Lessons,* p. 299. (Emphasis added.)
3. *The Desire of Ages,* p. 688.
4. *Testimonies,* vol. 5, pp. 539, 540.
5. Luke 17:17.
6. *Testimonies,* vol. 1, p. 704. (Emphasis added.)
7. Luke 17:15, 16.

Speak No Evil   pages 61 - 66

1. *Testimonies,* vol. 5, p. 59.
2. *Evangelism,* p. 634. (Emphasis added.)
3. *Testimonies,* vol. 1, p. 165.
4. *The Ministry of Healing,* p. 492.
5. *Testimonies,* vol. 8, p. 36.
6. *Sunshine Magazine,* August, 1963.
7. *Ibid.,* June, 1963.
8. John 8:7.
9. *Testimonies,* vol. 4, p. 196. (Emphasis added.)
10. *Sunshine Magazine,* May, 1963.
11. *Testimonies,* vol. 4, p. 196.
12. *Ibid.,* vol. 7, p. 183.
13. *Ibid.,* vol. 5, p. 242.
14. *Ibid.,* vol. 1, p. 145.
15. *Ibid.,* vol. 4, p. 194.
16. *Ibid.,* vol. 6, p. 151.
17. *Ibid.,* vol. 5, p. 274.
18. *Ibid.,* p. 488.
19. Ephesians 5:11, 12.

Not So Funny   pages 67 - 68

1. *Evangelism,* p. 636.
2. Ecclesiastes 10:1.

Practice What You Preach   pages 69 - 72

1. *Testimonies,* vol. 5, p. 460.
2. Frank S. Mead, in *Tarbell's Teachers' Guide for 1964.*
3. R. R. Hegstad, *Review and Herald,* April 8, 1965.
4. *Sunshine Magazine,* August, 1964.
5. Kenneth Wood, Jr., *Meditations for Moderns,* p. 78.
6. E. G. White, *General Conference Bulletin,* 1895, p. 438.

7. *Messages to Young People,* pp. 201, 202.

8. *Sunshine Magazine,* August, 1963.

9. *The Desire of Ages,* p. 142.

10. *The Ministry of Healing,* p. 470.

11. *Sunshine Magazine,* June, 1964.

12. John 1:4.

The Pessimist   pages 73 - 76

1. *Testimonies,* vol. 7, p. 244. (Emphasis added.)

2. Ella Wheeler Wilcox.

3. *Sunshine Magazine,* August, 1963.

4. *Ibid.*

5. *Patriarchs and Prophets,* p. 428.

6. Matthew 6:34

7. *Sunshine Magazine,* October, 1963.

8. *Testimonies,* vol. 6, p. 389.

Business Is More Than Business   pages 77 - 80

1. *Testimonies,* vol. 6, p. 424.

2. Kenneth Wood, Jr., *Review and Herald,* August 27, 1964.

3. Revelation 22:15.

4. *Testimonies,* vol. 4, p. 310.

5. *Sunshine Magazine,* October, 1963.

6. *Review and Herald,* May 20, 1965.

7. Luke 16:10.

8. *Testimonies,* vol. 1, p. 150

9. Matthew 17:27.

10. *Testimonies,* vol. 9, p. 21.

Position Seekers   pages 81 - 87

1. *Sunshine Magazine,* June, 1964.

2. *Testimonies,* vol. 6, pp. 432, 433.

3. Psalm 75:6, 7.

4. *The Ministry of Healing,* p. 477.

5. *Christ's Object Lessons,* p. 327.

6. *Testimonies,* vol. 2, p. 136.

7. Jeremiah 45:5.

8. *The Ministry of Healing,* pp. 476, 477.

9. *Testimonies,* vol. 5, p. 132. (Emphasis added.)

10. *The Ministry of Healing,* p. 476.

11. *Testimonies,* vol. 5, p. 56.

12. *Messages to Young People,* p. 36.

13. *Sunshine Magazine,* October, 1963.

14. Henry Ward Beecher.

IS. *The Ministry of Healing,* p. 477.

16. Kenneth Wood, Jr., *Meditations for Moderns,* p. 180.

17. *Evangelism,* p. 683. (Emphasis added.)

18. 1 Peter 5:6.

19. *Testimonies,* vol. 5, p. 461.

20. *Ibid.,* pp. 132, 133.

21. Author unknown.

Forgive   pages 88 - 90

1. Matthew 18:3.

2. Luke 23:34.

3. 1 John 4:11.

4. *Christ's Object Lessons,* p. 251.

5. Romans 5:8.

6. *The Desire of Ages,* p. 645.

7. Luke 6:37.

Do You Expect Too Much of Others?   pages 91 - 96

1. John 8:11.

2. *The Ministry of Healing,* p. 168.

3. *Ibid.*

4. *The Ministry,* May, 1964.

The Secret to Better Human Relations Now   pages 97 - 101

1. *Testimonies to Ministers,* p. 145.

2. *Education,* p. 18.

3. *Child Guidance,* pp. 267, 268.

4. *Evangelism,* p. 342.

5. Acts 10:38.

6. *Education,* p. 80.

7. *The Desire of Ages,* p. 362.

8. *Testimonies,* vol. 1, p. 527. (Emphasis added.)

9. *Ibid.,* vol. 7, p. 257.

10. *Ibid.,* vol. 1, p. 434.

11. *Ibid.,* vol. 7, p. 194.

12. *Ibid.,* vol. 6, p. 393.

13. *The Ministry of Healing,* p. 512.